The Expectant Gardener

Simone Martel

The Expectant Gardener

Simone Martel

CREATIVE ARTS BOOK COMPANY
Berkeley, California

For information contact:
Creative Arts Book Company
833 Bancroft Way
Berkeley, California 94710
(800) 848-7789

ISBN 0-88739-281-4 Paper
Library of Congress Catalog Number 99-63266
Printed in the United States of America

Illustrations by Susan Gaber, reproduced from *Treasury of Flower Designs*, Dover Publications, Inc., 1981.

Table of Contents

Introduction   xi

Chapter One—Some Gardens   1

The Big Garden in the Hills, 1 Looking Forward, 5
The Blake Estate, 6 Romance, 8 The Little Garden
in the Flats—The First Year, 8 A Window on the
Garden, 10 A House and its Garden, 12 A Closer
Look, 14 Starting to Learn, 16 Blissing Out at the
Home Improvement Center, 21 Spacing Out at the
Back of the Classroom, 23

Chapter Two—That Awkward Age   26

The Greedy Gardener, 26 The Fuchsia Border, 27
Sculpting Trees, 27 The Next Step, 28 Non-Sexist
Soil Improvement, 29 Liberty, 32 Panic in the
Garden, 33 Floury Borders, 34 Looking for Rules,
35 A Matter of Taste, 37 Intuition, 38 Changes, 39
The Wrong Plants, 40 The Second Winter, 41 Death,
42 Birth, 43 A Gardener, 43

Chapter Three—Finding the Right Plants   46

How to Make Traffic Island Plants Seem Glamorous,
46 Growing Up, Growing Upward, 50 Learning to
Use Unsociable Perennials, 51 Plotting the Third
Year, 53 Every Inch Counts, 55

Chapter Four—Sculpting A Garden   *56*

Using the Space, 56 An Island Bed, 57 The Pond, 58
Framing a View, 59 The Borders, 59 A Simple Path,
60 A Cheap Patio, 61 Hardscape That Says Too
Much, 62 The Pond, Take Two, 64 A Brazen
Fantasy, 66 The Lawn, 68 Meanwhile, in the Front
Yard, 71 The Pergola, 72 Pots, 73 A Rose Border,
74 The Greenhouse, 75 Finished?, 76

Chapter Five—Two Lessons   *78*

Stumbling Onward—The Fourth Year, 78 Focal
Points in the Borders, 79 The North Border: Semi-
Symmetry, 81 The South Border—Edible
Landscaping, 82 The Back Border—Abundance and
Restraint, 84 Transplanting, 86 Color Scheming, 87
Using Color in a Small Garden, 90 Progress, 92

Chapter Six—Time and the Garden   *93*

The Garden Ripens—The Fifth Year, 93
Camouflaging with Plants, 94 Time and the Frugal
Gardener, 95 Vanished, 96 Maintenance—The Sixth
and Seventh Years, 97 Renovation—The Eighth Year,
97

Chapter Seven—A Garden in the World   *101*

Our Ninth Spring in the Neighborhood, 101
Temptation, 102 Glorious Weather and Dismal
Gardens, 103 Reaching Out, 105 A Gathering Place,
106

Chapter Eight—Winter Rituals   *112*

The Tenth Year—A Specimen Year, 112 Conception,
113 A Snowy Garden, 114 Getting Dirty, 115
Springtime—Sort Of, 117 Hyacinths, 118 Crocuses,
119 In Quince-Blossom Time, 119 Sprouts, 120
Regarding Leaves, 123 Roses, 124 A Valentine's
Day Ritual, 124 Iceland Poppies, 126

Queasy Among the Calla Lilies, 126   The Colors of
Spring, 127   Blue Flowers, 129   Dutch Iris, 130
Mind the Gap, 130   Time to Set Out the Seedlings ,
132

Chapter Nine—One Spring Day   134

Mail Order Plants, 134   Seeds, 135   Saltines and
Snails, 137   Weeds, 139   City Birds, 141   A
Gardener's Body, 142   Of Dahlias and Feminism, 143
The Big and Small of It, 145

Chapter Ten—The Middle Months   147

Springtime in California, 147   Plump April, 148
Crazy for Corms, 149   Coralbells, 150   An Odd
Couple, 150   Prima Donnas and Supporting Players,
151   Perspective, 152   Hot Hot Hot, 153   Fed Up
with Foliage, 154   Delirious, 156   Bountiful
Blossoms, 158   Enjoying It All, 160   The Quickening,
160   Making Pictures, 160   The Stork Party, 162
Plums and Nectarines, 163

Chapter Eleven—Harvest   165

Fog and Sun, 165   Down on the Farm, 168
Tomatoes, 169   Vegetables Feed My Fantasies More
Than They Fill My Belly, 170   Summer Beauty,
Summer Bounty, 171   Chickens, Grape Vines and
Dusty Oleanders, 172   Obedient Plants and Lantanas:
A Late-Summer Duo, 173   Summer Annuals, 175
Autumn Eccentricity, 176   A Renaissance of Bugs and
Bloom, 177   Weeds and Other Aggravations, 178
One Question and Many Answers, 179   Yellow
Quinces, 182   The End, 183

Glossary   187

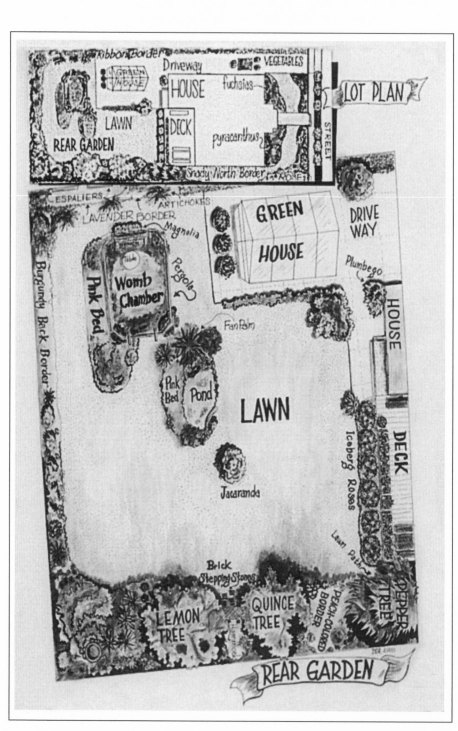

The Expectant Gardener

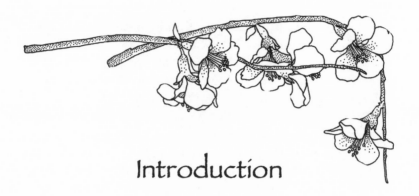

Introduction

This book was written for Leo, before he ever was Leo. Before I knew he would become Leo.

I wrote it when I was pregnant, to explain to my baby-to-be why his mother-to-be spent so much time in her garden.

The story began one morning in February when I was about six weeks pregnant. I was weeding near the pond—feeling tired and queasy, chomping on saltine crackers—when I happened to spot some scale insects dotting the twigs of a *Salvia greggii*. A moment later, I found the bud of a narcissus eaten through by a small slug. My response to this devastation was not very maternal. I cursed out loud, scraping the scale off the twig with my thumb nail and grinding the slug under the heel of my boot.

Then I wondered what my baby would think of its foul-mouthed, violent mother. Why such an impassioned reaction to a few brown polka dots and a small slimy creature? For that matter, why all this weeding and compost-spreading and moving around of perfectly nice plants from one part of the garden to the other? Why such commitment to a fairly ordinary back yard? Why this continual fussing and planning and puttering?

I pictured the embryo inside me, resting in the warmth and darkness, with nothing to do but grow. How it must marvel at my hyperactivity.

"What is she doing? Why on earth is she going to so much trouble over a few plants? Why does she want to make a garden? Most of all, what exactly *is* a garden?"

When I thought about the question from the baby's point of view, I began to wonder, too.

My garden was important to me. I knew that much. And I was pretty sure it would be important to my baby. After all, the place would make up a large part of my baby's world. I imagined my newborn in October lying beside me in a carrier while I dug holes for bulbs, or performed other late-autumn tasks. Then I pictured spring, and my baby crawling across the lawn, maybe pausing under the lemon tree to look up at a squirrel.

The scene boggled my mind. I had as much trouble imagining the baby as I had in believing that the powdery lobelia seed I held in the palm of my hand would eventually grow into enough frothy, plants to edge the peach-colored border. "Eventually" was the key word here. I had so much time to wait. From February to October. The growing season in my California garden. One entire year, minus the three months of rain and cold. An agonizingly long time.

So I had plenty of opportunity to work out the story of my garden. I thought it up in installments, like a soap opera. At first, I didn't write it down on paper or compose the story on a computer screen. Instead, I puzzled it out in the garden. I imagined it and dreamed it and muttered every word of it while weeding sour grass out of the mixed borders and lugging buckets of manure tea across the lawn. When I wasn't arguing with the pugnacious Cecile Brunner rose, or grumbling at a floppy bachelor's button, my lips moved, spelling out what I was doing and why I was doing it.

I had a lot to explain. So many plants growing, blooming, fading, sometimes blooming again. So many tasks. So many decisions. I never had realized before how much my small garden contains.

Later in the year, I started to write down my thoughts, because I wanted to retain something of those months of reflection and anticipation and growth. Of course, once I began writing, new ideas bubbled up.

I wrote about the two gardens I had loved as a child long before I had a garden of my own: my parents' garden and an estate garden I often visited as a teenager. Those two places shaped my notion of what a garden can be.

I described the difficult process of making my own garden—a frustrating project, because I started out horticulturally ignorant, despite my long-time passion for other people's gardens. I also wrote about the decade of the garden's development, the ten years between the garden's formation and my own baby's conception.

I found myself turning mentally away from my baby and wondering about the experiences of other gardeners. "How do other gardeners think about their gardens?" I asked myself. "And how do they define their roles as gardeners?" I was especially curious about whether they sometimes feel maternal (or paternal) as they plant and weed and prune and transplant and gently shape their back yards into beautiful, harmonious gardens.

"Perhaps they don't," I decided. "Maybe some gardeners feel absolutely the opposite way. Maybe they see themselves as children in Mother Nature's lap, learning from nature and adapting themselves to its laws."

I wondered about myself, too. What was my role? And where does the part I play place me in relation to plants, insects, birds, the weather, my husband, my parents, my neighbors, the world at large?

These ruminations sometimes carried me far away from my own garden. No matter how far my thoughts took me, though, Leo remained at the center. Even though Leo is not a gardener—yet—he was my reason for writing this book and my reason for considering all this to begin with.

The idea of writing a book for a baby may seem sentimental, but I don't believe the story is. After all, there's nothing really sentimental about babies—or gardens. They're both too real. The "growth" I measured that year was real, too, and not merely spiritual. I measured it by the ajuga creeping along the front of the border, and by the boltonia shooting up in back. I also measured it by my own growth, as the grubby green sundress I wore for gardening began to stretch tighter and tighter around my middle.

In most respects, that growing season was like any other. The part of Northern California, where I garden, has a Mediterranean climate, with a rainy period that runs, usually, from September to April. The seasons do not heed the calendar. Spring comes early, sometimes as early as February. Summer is foggy and cool. We enjoy our warmest days in September and even October.

A hard frost strikes about once every five years. When it does, only the toughest, most established hibiscus, bougainvillea, and other tropical plants survive. Dahlia tubers and other tender bulbs sometimes die, too. These frosts always take us by surprise, reminding us bluntly that we live in Northern, not Southern, California.

Nevertheless, the growing season is long. Daffodils bloom in the first warm days of February, tomato plants often bear fruit into November, and weeds flourish in every month of the year. There is never time to oil the tools and set them aside. In this climate, the chores never end.

At times, the year I was pregnant, the repetitious tasks exasperated me; at other times, I found the routine soothing. Of course, the little crises and triumphs kept me interested, as always.

In one big way, though, that year was different. While I performed the usual jobs, often barely thinking about what my hands were doing, the question of "why" preoccupied my mind. "Why make a garden?"

The answer, I have found, is complex, the reasons spreading outward like roots.

Here are those roots—untangled as best I could.

Chapter One
Some Gardens

The Big Garden in the Hills

My parents had a large garden in the Berkeley hills. For me it was a whole world, shrunk down to my size. It contained some of everything. There was a sunny plot where my father grew vegetables to use in his health-food recipes. There were enormous rocks for climbing and some terraces blooming with iris and roses and hollyhocks. A small lawn capped the hill between two great holly bushes. When I stood there, I could look out at the San Francisco Bay and count three bridges.

The sun was wonderful. I don't remember any fog. I used to take my frozen orange juice popsicles and sit right on the ground in the middle of the main patio, feeling the hot cement burn through my skirt, and watching drops of juice fall on the pavement and shrink away.

There was a shady area in my parents' garden too. The paths wound down among scrub oaks to a second, shadowy patio surrounded by informal beds of acanthus and Japanese anemone and ferns and lots of ivy. Sometimes I heard rats rustling in the leaves.

Nestled at the bottom of the garden was a rental house where an English professor lived. Once I came upon him sunbathing nude on his deck. For a moment I gawked through the ferns at his big white body. Then I raced back up the path, running barefoot over prickly oak leaves.

Friends often visited me in my garden. When I was seven, my mother built a playhouse out of scrap lumber. When it was finished, my playmates and I arranged our tea sets on a little table by its curtained window. I don't remember hosting any tea parties, though. Instead, my friends and I performed elaborate experiments with bean plants and colored water and spit and pee and unfortunate worms dug out of the compost pit.

Because I was an only child, I also played by myself a lot. That was when the garden became most important to me. My black cat, Sylvia, kept me company during those solitary hours. When we were alone, she grew into a huge panther and I became a witch. In an old saucepan, I mixed a foul brew of rose hips, leaf mould, smashed snails, oak moths with wiry feelers, red-orange pyracantha berries, acorns, pill bugs, and sometimes my own blood.

To me, the witch's brew symbolized the garden's mysterious power. I loved that power. I never believed that the garden should be all sunny and flowery and spick-and-span. I knew instinctively that the garden was a whole world and that decomposition was as much a part of that world as growth, that foulness could be as compelling as beauty. I wanted it that way. I would not have loved the sunny garden without the shady area nearby. I would not have cared for the pale green new leaves without the old brown leaves rotting underneath.

As I stirred the brew, I felt connected to the garden's dark, brooding, secret magic. Sex and birth. Life and death. Food and excrement. Rain and sun. They were all there in that garden.

Once, I asked my mother if our oak trees were very old. She answered that they were old enough to have given shade to the Native Americans who lived in the Berkeley hills long before houses and gardens covered the land. That thrilled me. When I touched the trees I felt close to something old.

After that, I often pretended to be an Indian girl. I couldn't meet the Ohlone children of two hundred years ago, so I became one myself. It was a very private game. The Indian girl I pretended to be was even more solitary than the witch had been, for she had no friends at all, not even a pet panther. I made believe that she was the last of her tribe, living on the edge of society.

I played this game often, but one occasion in particular stands out. It was an unusually warm evening, and I lay hidden among the California poppies on the hillside below the lawn. As the dusk deepened, I felt the neighborhood draw in. The boys next door came home from school and played basketball outside while they waited for their dinner. I could hear them grunting and laughing and sometimes shouting while the ball thump-thumped in their driveway.

The writer in the house behind ours had been tapping on his typewriter all afternoon. Now the typewriter fell silent and the writer came out onto his porch to smoke a cigarette. I couldn't see him, but I could smell his cigarette. I could also smell my own dinner cooking.

I lay motionless on the hillside among the poppies, until the sun slipped behind Mount Tamalpias across the bay and the lights came on in the houses around me. Eventually the pounding of basketball next door stopped, and the boys went in to eat. The writer threw away his cigarette butt and went away, too.

Then I turned my attention toward my own house. I could see a lamp glowing in the dining room. My mother came to the window to pull the curtains. When I saw her face, I played a spooky little game. "Who is that woman?" I asked myself, pretending not to know. "I wonder who else lives with her. I wonder what it's like to live in that big brown house." I almost convinced myself that I was a stranger.

I felt separate from my own life inside that house, but I felt close to the garden. I felt close to the ground under me and the plants around me. I even felt close to the pill bugs trundling around the poppy stems. With my eyes half closed, I let the ants crawl on my hands and up my arms. That evening, I felt that I knew the bugs in the garden better than I knew my own parents.

After a while, my father called me in for dinner.

"We saw you lying there on the ground," he said, as he brought the food to the table.

I climbed into my chair silently. "So, I wasn't hidden after all," I thought.

"You didn't seem to be having much fun," my mother added. "Weren't you bored?"

They seemed so insensitive to the mystery and power in their own yard. Sometimes, I could hardly believe it was their garden, too.

It was, of course. They did all the work.

At the time, I never thought about all the labor my parents put into the garden. The garden was mine. What did they have to do with it? In retrospect, I am impressed. The place must have required an enormous amount of effort.

My father did the heavy chores, pulling ivy, slashing blackberry vines, digging bamboo out of the rose bed. Not very interesting to a ten-year-old. My mother was more fun to garden with because she puttered. I spent many of my happiest hours in the garden puttering along beside her.

It was very companionable. I would make witch's brew or build tiny houses of leaves and sticks, while she did whatever it was grownups did. Probably she weeded. Or maybe she deadheaded, removing dead or dying blossoms from her plants. I wish I had paid attention, but the mechanics of gardening were not important to me yet.

I made a game out of our camaraderie and called it "Hansel and Gretel." I pretended that my mother was my big brother and that our parents had abandoned us in the middle of an oak forest. We had to eat nuts and berries and sleep in a shack built of bark (my playhouse). I loved this game. My mother and I played it for years. Or rather, I did. While my mother puttered, I gathered those nuts and berries and plotted our survival.

As far as I was concerned, the heartless forces of nature ruled the garden. The garden was anti-civilization. It was untamed, a dangerous place, but one where I belonged. My room—with my toys and books and stuffed animals—was safe and dull by comparison. It did not mean much to me. When I was unhappy, I did not go and throw myself onto my bed. I always ran outside with my grief.

Looking Forward

Twenty years later, I marvel at the idea that my own garden—a little rectangular plot—will take its place in a whole new set of memories. I ask myself, "Twenty years from now, will my child remember playing near me while I puttered among the roses? Will he think back to the times when he hid behind the smokebush, or collected nasturtium pods for playfood, or watched a hummingbird dart among the fuchsias?"

I look around the yard, and wonder what aspects of this garden will intrigue Leo—or scare him, or enchant him? What parts will haunt him? Will the greenhouse seem cobwebby and mysterious? Will the pond seem green and infinitely deep?

The eight-by-ten-foot greenhouse, built from a kit, contains no mystery for me. I know it too well. And I know every inch of that pond, because I dug it myself. But maybe my child will find magic in my garden, as I used to find it in my parents' garden.

As an adult, I have discovered a new way to enjoy a garden. Instead of wandering through an enchanted space, I have learned to create that enchantment myself. That means deadheading and weeding and spraying for bugs. In some ways, the fun is less complete, less perfect, but it's also less passive. My garden has awakened new emotions in me, feelings of responsibility and pride.

Frankly, I prefer the garden I have now. The garden in the hills was never quite mine. I camped out in it, I hid in it, I prowled around it, but my parents planted it and tended it. It really was theirs, no matter what I thought at the time.

It is better to be an adult, really. Not only can I eat what I like (no mackerel casserole with wheat germ sprinkled on top), and wear what I like (no tie-dye), I can also plant what I like. That means no pink-and-white-striped petunias. (My mother loved them, but they always looked fake to me.) And no eggplant. (My father cooked the beautiful purple fruits into vats of slimy mousaka.)

Making my own garden also means growing plenty of forget-me-nots, plumbago, and blue-flowering agapanthus, for I missed blue flowers when I grew up. My mother wouldn't tolerate them. She still winces when she passes the pots of trailing lobelia on my front porch.

"But it's *my* garden," I think. "Ha!"

That's one advantage of growing up.

The Blake Estate

When I was teenager, my parents sold the house in the hills and moved to a smaller place in the flats, on a wide busy street. My parents missed the bay view, but I didn't. What I missed was the seclusion, the sense of being in my own world.

The front garden at the new house was fairly large, but not private. I longed for a spot away from my parents, away from the groan and wheeze of buses, and away from the strangers who were always hurrying up and down the sidewalk. I was already a self-conscious adolescent. In the garden of our new house, I felt perpetually on display.

Eventually, I gave up on the new garden and found somewhere else to go. Returning to the hills we had left, I discovered a wonderful place called the Blake Estate.

The president of the University of California at Berkeley lives at the Blake Estate, but I didn't know that back then. I went to see the garden, not the president. It was open to the public, but nearly always empty. To me it was like going home to my childhood garden in the hills, and finding it five times as large and fifty times more beautiful. After I discovered the Blake Estate, I went back up from the flat land regularly to visit its garden.

I didn't go there looking for a place to play, for I was no longer a solitary child involved in private games. I was a politically aware teenager—an *anxious* teenager—and I went to the garden looking for solace. During those years, I was terrified that the United States or the Soviet Union ("the evil empire") was going blow up the world. The threat seemed very real to me. At fourteen and fifteen I worried far more about bombs than I did about boys or grades.

I needed a place to calm down. The Blake garden became my place.

I wandered all over the four-acre estate, from the shady redwood canyon, to the sunny yellow garden, bright with potentilla, and slipper flower (*Calceolaria integrifolia* 'Golden Nugget'). At the time, I couldn't have named any of the plants I found inside the garden. (I have gone back since then to jot down the names and take note of my favorites.) Back then, I simply loved them all.

I returned most often to the Italianate water garden in front of the house. I loved that place with a kind of piety. As I neared the pool, my pace slowed and my motions grew dignified. I watched water dripping into a mossy basin, and became focused and clearheaded. I gazed along the *allée* of evergreen magnolias, and felt rational.

The formal landscape reminded me of my sanity, and that was why I cherished it. The world seemed less out of control when I walked among reflecting pools and trimmed yew hedges. After half an hour in that green place, my heart seemed to beat differently.

The Blake Estate taught me that a formal garden can have as much strength as a wild one, although at the time, I didn't realize how that could be so. The philosophy of landscape design was far from my mind. Lately, though, I've compared my parents' naturalistic garden in the hills to the stately Blake garden. I've thought about the way those two gardens touched me and gave me something of themselves. In the end, I've come to believe that a successful garden, in *any* style, has the power to influence moods and touch emotions.

Romance

Then two more years passed, and I changed again. I was seventeen and in love. I craved sunny terraces and lavish flowers and spicy-smelling herbs. I didn't want to run wild in a garden like a solitary deer, as I had when I was eight. Nor did I want to stroll calmly down elegant gravel paths, as I had at fifteen. I wanted to be romantic, in a romantic garden. And again, I found what I was looking for at the Blake Estate.

I took my boyfriend to the garden. But with him, I walked right past the formal grounds. Half-unconsciously, I sought out the most sensuous spot in the whole estate. I led him down to the Mediterranean hillside garden below the house.

On warm spring afternoons, Paul and I lay together on the lawn, surrounded by manzanita and verbena. We looked up at the sky and breathed in the warm, lavender-scented air. Those afternoons were bliss. Often at four-thirty, when the garden closed, an embarrassed gardener had to roust us from our spot on the lawn. If he hadn't, we never would have gone home.

The Little Garden in the Flats—The First Year

So far, I had been a very idle lover-of-gardens. But eventually Paul and I married and bought a home of our own, with a little yard in back. (Leo wouldn't come until much later; it would be about ten years before we considered starting a family.) Now that I had some land of my own, I could no longer lie on the grass and dream. I had to get off my back and start working.

Only, I didn't know how. I enjoyed gardens, I felt vibrantly alive in gardens, but I knew nothing about how to grow a plant or design a landscape. Gardens were always sets for my personal dramas; someone else did the work. My mother and father tended our yard at home, doing something or other with clippers and trowels. A gang of university students and employees kept the Blake garden immaculate. So I knew nothing about how a garden becomes a garden. I certainly had never contemplated making a garden of my own. But I thought it might be fun to try.

In the weeks before we gained possession of the property, when Paul and I still lived in my parents' basement, I often daydreamed about the wonderful landscape I would create in our new back yard. I didn't bother to learn anything about the technicalities of gardening; I worked in the realm of fantasy. The landscape in my imagination grew more and more grandiose by the day.

Then the bubble popped. Paul and I revisited our new property one evening when it was still in escrow. We couldn't go inside the house until it became officially ours, but we could peek through all the windows, and sit for a while on the wooden deck behind the kitchen.

"I'd forgotten how small it is," I said, eyeing the weedy yard, enclosed by a six-foot redwood fence. In my memory, it had spread into something more impressive. "I guess I won't have to learn to garden after all."

I could not imagine making anything wonderful out of that boxy little space. I was spoiled. To me a garden meant half an acre, at least. A garden meant the Blake Estate or my parents' garden in the hills. Or it meant a country property featured in one of my mother's glossy lifestyle magazines. When I remembered those luscious color photographs I had seen of "the owner tying up the roses on the old cottage wall," I was convinced that our own tiny yard could never be a proper garden.

Also, our new place was very urban—very different from those country retreats in the magazines. The neighborhood crowded close around the redwood fence. We could hear lives being lived in a dozen houses. Dishes clattered. Radios murmured. Kids shouted. Dogs barked. When we looked up, we could see the Bay Area Rapid Transit train gliding above our neighbors' rooftops with its load of commuters. And from the front porch, we could see a drug dealer standing at the street corner.

The yard was too small and too urban to be a proper garden. I was also probably too young and too poor to be a proper gardener. I'd been silly even to contemplate it. The gardeners in those magazine articles were always rich and over forty.

So several months passed before I again thought seriously of starting a garden.

A Window on the Garden

Even if I had wanted to begin a garden sooner, I wouldn't have been able to find the money or the time. Paul and I spent all the cash we could scrape together on paint, spackling compound, and putty knives. After we gained possession of the house, we spent two months working on it before we moved in.

The previous owner hadn't bothered to fix up the house before selling it. We found old mousetraps in the bedroom and a tequila bottle in the freezer. The five rooms were shabby and stark, painted a cold white, and decorated with scuff marks and grubby hand prints.

We finally moved into our house in late December. Our repairs were nowhere near finished but we moved in anyway, because we wanted to spend Christmas in our own home.

That first morning, I woke feeling disoriented and slightly depressed. The bedroom looked bleak in the wintery light, and the cracks in the walls seemed alarmingly wide. The night before, I had seen a spider creep out of a hole in the plaster. Or thought I had.

Groggily, I wandered into the tiny bathroom, showered, dressed, and then opened the frosted window. At that moment, my feelings toward the weedy backyard began to change. I noticed that some of those weeds were actually pretty weeds. More than that, I realized that the overall space had a nice feeling. Maybe because the house felt so dreary that morning, the yard shone by contrast.

I felt like Dorothy after the tornado, peering out of my black-and-white house at a technicolor landscape. Bright orange California poppies dotted the entire yard. Golden nasturtiums billowed among the poppies. Purple morning glory vines climbed the fence and engulfed a neglected pyracantha. Onion grass raised white, bell-like flowers on succulent green stems. To complete the picture, a magnificent crop of dandelions added a sprinkling of yellow.

The plot of weeds looked like a meadow in bloom. Of course, I could not see the nasty blackberry vines twisting in the shadows beneath the nasturtiums. And I did not know about the creeping crab grass, either. Nor could I imagine how many hours I would spend digging up onion grass bulbs and tugging out dandelions. All I knew was that the overgrown backyard was *alive*. I could smell life in the moist, faintly onion-scented air.

I had spent time in my garden before, of course. Paul and I always ate our sandwiches out there—even on the coldest days—just for a chance to get the smell of paint out of our noses for a while. I even had pulled a few weeds, experimentally. But I never had woken up to the garden before. I never had seen it in the morning light. I never had looked out a window at it, casually, matter-of-factly, and realized, with a wonderful shock, that I owned that yard and it would be there three-hundred and sixty-five days a year, and that every morning I could open my bathroom window after my shower and look at it while I dried my hair.

The house—its foundation under my feet and its roof over my head, its lath-and-plaster walls, its pipes and wiring, and all the bits and pieces of it that needed work—formed our shelter and our investment. We had to get them into good condition. That mattered. The garden did not matter. The house, however, was dead; the garden was alive.

That morning, looking out the window, I felt intensely just how full of life that small garden was. And I understood that, along with the house, I had bought worms, spiders, caterpillars, ants, and a living piece of earth. It was a piece of the world that just happened to have a fence around it and just happened to belong to me. And I felt responsible.

Even though the burden of the house should have weighed on me more, it didn't. When I considered all the life flourishing in the garden, it seemed like a far more important place than a sagging five-room house.

It was also a beautiful place, I realized that morning. Even in its neglected state, there was something in that yard. I could not have described what that something was, but I could tell that the garden was a good place. I forgot that I ever had thought gardeners had to be rich or middle aged. I lost my heart to that patch of ground.

A House and Its Garden

Since that first morning, I've often leaned out the bathroom window. I probably have spent hours standing there, doing nothing, just looking out. In some ways, a garden looks best that way—glimpsed from between curtains or through a doorway.

A garden could exist all by itself, I suppose. A dedicated gardener could make a garden in a clearing in the woods or on a mountaintop. But I suspect such isolated gardens are rare.

Usually, the garden lies near a house. In fact, the garden usually exists because of the house. A garden is really nothing more than the ground left over after a house has been built, a margin of unused earth stretching between a building and a fence or another building. At least, it is until you make it into something more.

During those first months in my own home, I thought a lot about the relationship between a house and its garden. I thought about the house and garden I had just bought, and I thought about other house-and-gardens I had known.

I never had been inside the Italianate mansion at the Blake Estate. I never even had glimpsed a face in a window. Nevertheless, the presence of the house influenced my experience of the garden. Even though I never saw anyone in the windows, I always suspected that someone was there, watching me. Maybe the house itself was watching me through those huge plate-glass windows.

I didn't mind feeling watched. Maybe I even found the experience exciting. But the existence of the un-entered, un-enterable house, with its big staring windows, always emphasized the fact that the garden was not mine.

As for my parents' house in the hills, I always pretended that the house and garden were unrelated. I imagined that the garden was a far-off wilderness, probably because that was what I wanted it to be. Like most children, I wanted to get as far away from my parents as possible.

In retrospect, though, I realized that the house complemented the garden quite well. The dark and sober interior balanced the exuberant plantings outside.

I remembered hot summer days when I left my friends playing tag on the lawn and galloped inside by myself—all sweaty and tangle-haired and rumpled—pausing, just inside the kitchen door, to enjoy the weird otherness of the familiar room.

On those days, the house felt like a museum, cool and still and remote. It appeared purple-dark to my sun dazzled eyes; and silent, except for the hum of the refrigerator and the sound of my own quick breathing. After gulping down a glass of water from the kitchen tap, I raced back out into a garden that seemed brighter, under a sun that seemed hotter. I enjoyed the summer day more after that, because I had come to it out of a dark, quiet house.

My parents' house was a shelter in the wilderness, coolness in heat, silence in noise. I could tell as soon as I moved into my tiny, sunny house that living there would be a very different experience. "This place is *transparent*," I said to Paul. "It's all windows and glass doors. Do you realize that from several places outside, you can actually see through the house—in one side and out the other?"

Right from the beginning, the line in our new home between indoors and outdoors blurred. As soon as the weather warmed, Paul and I set up our dining table on the deck. All through spring and summer and well into fall, we stayed outdoors as much as possible.

When I dashed into the house to answer the phone or refill my coffee cup, I never had that sense of ducking into a cool dim cave. The windows were always open. A bee usually circled in the air near the ceiling. A few cats slept on the furniture (the others were outside, sleeping on the patio furniture). Jars of flowers on the window sills brought the outdoors inside. And everywhere, the sun blazed through the curtainless windows.

Eventually, the house stopped seeming dingy. I came to love it almost as much as I loved the garden. I loved them together. I loved the way the indoor space melted into the outdoor space, as though there were no difference between the two.

A Closer Look

After I chopped back the blackberry canes and tore the morning glory vines off the pyracantha, I paced around my new garden, getting to know the place. The south side was sunny, with a driveway running the length of the house and ending at an old, collapsing garage in the back yard. Across from the garage, on the north side of our back yard, four trees of varying size crowded close to the fence.

An overgrown lemon tree and a shrubby quince grew together in a tangle. They clearly needed pruning. I made a mental note. A beautiful California pepper tree shaded the deck. The pepper tree was perfect as it was. Two feet away from the pepper tree, though, an acacia tree—probably self-sown—towered up fifty feet.

Despite the trees, the yard was basically sunny. A nice space. But quite flat. Boxy. Potentially boring. The space was without mystery. And the deck—though spacious and well-built—added to the dullness.

At that time, the wooden deck outside the kitchen door really did seem like the deck of a ship on which you stood like a captain surveying the sea. (The sea, of course, was the sea of weeds that stretched from the garage on one side of the yard to the trees on the other side.) There were no paths, no places to walk to, and nothing hidden. There was no reason for the captain to climb down from the deck and investigate. I knew from the start that I would have to obscure the view with trees and tall plants. And I would need to tempt the captain off his perch by giving him paths to walk on, paths that led him somewhere. But I had very little idea of how to accomplish this.

The garden overwhelmed me a little. Strangely, it didn't seem so small any more. The longer I looked at it, the bigger it seemed to get. Compared to gardens in books and magazines, it was tiny of course. But for the neighborhood, it was actually rather big. The area we had moved into was so densely populated that many homeowners had converted their houses into duplexes or triplexes. Other homeowners had built rental cottages in their back yards. Some had even turned remodeled garages into rental units.

Our house was much too small to convert to units, and our garage was falling down, but a cottage would have fit neatly into the back yard. So we had got our hands on something quite unusual for that neighborhood—a patch of under-utilized earth.

Very few cultivated plants grew there. And the ones that were there seemed to be mostly thorns. A narrow side yard led from the back yard to the front yard. Unlike the south side, with its sunny driveway, this side was shady, crowded with acanthus, sword ferns and prickly, rambling, asparagus ferns. In the front yard, three ancient and barbed pyracantha shrubs crowded up against the bedroom window. Above them, an enormous Cecile Brunner rose grew in a twenty-foot tidal wave, curving up over the roof. A straw-colored bougainvillaea—long-dead, but still thorny—grew against the front porch.

I didn't think all those spikes could be coincidental. The plants, I decided, were not there to be beautiful. They were meant to discourage burglars.

The front yard also was home to a few thornless plants. Under the living-room window, on the south side of the front yard, an old woody fuchsia bloomed meagerly on long, unpruned stems beside an enormous jade plant in a cracked plastic tub. Some calla lilies had escaped from the neighbor's garden, and a great clump of them were plowing their way through the Bermuda grass across our front yard. But besides that, nothing lived there but weeds.

My mother told me I should be glad not to have inherited someone else's garden. After eight years in a new house, she was still trying to create a yellow-and-white garden in a back yard dominated by three huge pink camellias planted by the previous owner. My mother hated the color of the camellias, but she could not bring herself to cut down such fine, large trees. Every spring hundreds of self-sown purple cineraria sprouted around the bases of the camellias, adding to her troubles. Naturally, she couldn't bear to pull up such exuberant free-blooming flowers, either. In the end, she planted her yellow abutilon in the back of the border and her yellow daffodils in the front, and pretended not to notice the intrusion of purple and pink in the middle.

She told me I was lucky that no previous gardener with an affection for magenta and grape haunted my garden. She said that what I had was not a garden at all. It was a potential garden.

From that first morning at the bathroom window, my potential garden drew me in. When I needed a break from spackling and painting, I wandered outside, putty knife in hand, to contemplate the colorful, unstructured space.

Paul's interest in our new house ended at the back door (which he fitted with new weatherstripping and painted cream). The yard was mine: trees, rocks, bugs, mud—all that seething potential. Gardening, I felt sure, was about beginnings, about promise, about hope. I was interested in unfolding that promise.

But I had no practical knowledge. And "hope" alone was not enough. Not when paired with inexperience. What I needed now, was information.

Starting to Learn

Looking back, I can hardly believe I was so ignorant. For someone who had spent a lot of time in gardens, I knew nothing about plants. My ignorance so overwhelmed me, that I was almost too intimidated to start learning. I had told Paul, though, to expect a wonderful garden, come summer, so I had to do something. My first act was to head for the library.

At that time, Paul and I were still in college, so naturally we approached everything through books. The library seemed like the right place to go to if I wanted to learn something new. Perhaps in a different world, I might have asked my neighbors for advice. Or if I had been a different kind of person, I might have asked my mother for help. In fact, I did ask my mother, but not at the beginning.

That night, after my trip to the library, I took a botanical encyclopedia to bed with me and read it straight through, while Paul studied for a history exam beside me. This was not a good way for me to begin.

For one thing, the encyclopedia's small line drawings offered no sense of scale. The spiky blue blooms of the ajuga on page four and the blue delphinium spires on page thirteen looked exactly alike to me. I had to flip back and forth between the pages, and work my way through the dense little write-ups next to the pictures, in order to figure out that ajuga and delphiniums differ slightly in height.

The facts I managed to pick up from that encyclopedia rattled around in my head like sunflower seeds in a jar. I simply didn't know how to focus on all that new data.

"This is going to be difficult," I told myself. My confusion over the ajuga and delphiniums embarrassed me—the difference between the two plants seemed so obvious once I had figured it out. But the process of figuring it out was not simple. I could tell I was going to make a lot of mistakes before the season was over.

Paul, who was reading his history notes, interrupted my brooding. "What was the date of the treaty of Westphalia?" he challenged me.

"Don't bother me with European history now," I said, "I'm learning something hard."

I turned to the back of the encyclopedia and read the General Information. It was very interesting. "Listen, Paul.

There are two kinds of plants, perennials and annuals," I announced, as though I had made a remarkable discovery.

I hadn't got as far as biennials yet—that was in the second paragraph. But I had to share every bit of information with Paul as soon as I learned it. For some reason, as I bestowed my knowledge on him, I felt marginally less stupid myself.

In the beginning, I was a cerebral gardener. Once I got the concept of annuals and perennials (and biennials) down pretty well, I moved on to color schemes and plant heights and blooming times. Gradually, the information began to baffle me less, and I became a junkie.

I read all the books in the library (except the single-plant ones, such as *Know Your Cacti*) and started hanging out in the gardening sections of the bookstores, going dizzy with the effort of trying to read a twenty pound coffee table book standing up.

Paul said my relish for garden information reminded him of when I took Human Anatomy and Physiology in high school and used to entertain him on our dates by rattling off the names of the bones and muscles. Now, though, I was going on about ammonium sulfate and ammonium nitrate, about soil structure and the relative sizes of soil particles.

Paul was right. I loved knowing stuff. And here was a whole new body of knowledge—new to me, at least. I found out that potatoes belong to the deadly nightshade family and that green potatoes are poisonous. I learned that "precocious" does not always refer to Mozart, but can also refer to a star magnolia—which sprouts its flowers before its leaves—but never to my quince tree, which does not.

Most of the facts I gobbled up were fun and trivial. But I absorbed a few serious lessons, too. I started to understand how the natural world works. I started to think about flowers setting seed and decomposing; about compost feeding the soil. I started to think about how nothing goes away.

That first year, while I was still working out a garden design, I put in a temporary vegetable plot in the back yard.

It was like everybody's first garden, with several clumps of strawberry plants, some lettuce, snow peas, a few sparse rows of carrots, and lots of pansies around the edges. But I found wisdom even in that ordinary garden.

When I irrigated my strawberry plants, I thought about how the water I was splattering over the ground had run through pipes all the way from the melting snowpack in the Sierra Nevada. And as the water soaked into the earth around the berry plants, I imagined the roots taking in that water. Then, as time passed and the fruit grew big, I thought of the water making them swell. And when I picked the strawberries and ate them, and the juice dripped down my chin, I thought, "There's that water again. Nothing ever goes away."

This insight prompted me to garden organically, right from the start. Even without much imagination, I could pic-ture malathion sticking around as persistently as the water.

So when aphids curled the leaves of the strawberry plants, I checked my urge to spray. Instead I waited and watched joyfully as ladybugs discovered the infested plants. Beady-eyed, I squatted in the dirt, admiring the way a greedy ladybug crammed a soft green aphid into her mouth, and then inched along the dark green leaves, her front legs wag-gling, reaching for another mouthful.

The aphids never completely disappeared, but in time the pests and the predators achieved a balance. It was a bal-ance that struck me as magical.

To experienced gardeners, the revelations I experienced that first spring must seem naive, even pedestrian. Garden-ers are familiar with the balance of nature and take that miraculous interconnectedness for granted. But these things were not at all obvious to a twenty-one-year-old English lit-erature student who had previously spent most of her time in libraries and dark cafes.

My whole way of seeing changed. Absolutely nothing looked the same to me any more. My altered sensibility added a new element to my relationship with Paul. We still could examine a poem together, but we couldn't look at a flower with the same eyes. We didn't see alike. For instance, he couldn't tell a zinnia from a dahlia. That didn't matter in itself. I didn't even like zinnias very much, and only grew them the first year because they were easy to start from seed. What mattered was why he could not distinguish between the plants.

I realized that it was because he saw only the *flowers*. When I looked at a zinnia, I remembered the little narrow seed I had planted in a peat pot. When I saw a dahlia I thought of the almond-shaped tuber buried in the ground. So for me the difference was obvious: I didn't just see the plant, I saw the process.

All gardeners see this way. But I was new to the experience and therefore more self-conscious. Gardeners, I came to realize, hold the whole year in their minds. In February, they might look at hollyhock seedlings and imagine the plants in June, blooming eight feet tall at the back of the border. Or they might visualize those same hollyhocks in July, when the blossoms have faded and the round, dry seedpods are splitting open and releasing their disk-shaped seed. Optimistic gardeners might imagine volunteer seedlings sprouting next to the old stalks. Pessimistic gardeners might visualize rust growing on those seedlings.

With looking, comes judging. Gardeners are great judges. Say some of those hollyhocks have pink frilly, "powderpuff" flowers, and the rest are single flowers, of a deep black-purple (*Alcea rosea* 'Nigra'). Most gardeners could tell you —emphatically—which flower is lovelier. Opinions vary. But whatever our individual judgements, gardeners are the same—we cannot perceive without prejudice.

Nongardeners are less critical. To Paul, all flowers are pretty—because all flowers are pretty much the same. He doesn't take any pride in making considered distinctions, and he certainly doesn't lug along volumes of information inside his head, as I do. That makes his experience more direct—but poorer, I think. I like my complicated response to the simplest daisy (And what *is* a daisy? *Chrysanthemum frutescens*? *Coreopsis verticillata*? *Echinacea purpurea*? *Boltonia asteroides*? All these are daisies, says Paul, grandly. And when I object, he accuses me of nitpicking.)

In college, when I started hauling gardening books in my book bag, along with my *Norton Anthology of English Literature*, Paul told me he couldn't relate to this new side of me. He knew the other side, the English major, the woman who packed champagne and a hardback edition of the *Collected Yeats* for a hike to the beach. If he had thought a bit more he would have realized that the part of me that loved poetry was also the part of me that loved gardens.

I didn't actually spend all my time with my face stuck in twenty pound gardening books. It only seemed that way to Paul because I was always quoting from those books. I actually spent lots of time out in the garden with my hands on a trowel and my face close to stems and leaves and twigs and buds. But I didn't talk about that. What was there to say? That aspect of gardening was mindless and of the moment. Those moments were often perfect, but I couldn't describe that perfection.

The how-to stuff was easy to talk about. I chattered about the nitty-gritty details because that was the way I articulated my love for plants and landscape design. But all the time, potent feelings remained just that—feelings. Too murky to shape into thoughts, much less into words.

I had been close to my mother in our garden in the hills. I had been close to Paul at the Blake Estate. I had also been close to myself in these gardens. I could never forget that.

Blissing-Out at the Home Improvement Center

In a funny way, my garden brought me close to my mother for a second time. I had lost touch with her about the same time I lost interest in gardens. When I started high school, I decided that things in books mattered more than things in the ground. My mother must have decided I was a snob, because she withdrew from me then. So I tended to talk to my father, instead. Now I was back in the garden, literally and metaphorically and I found my mother there, not my father.

My father liked my garden well enough—as a backdrop, a stage set, a pleasant place for conversation. But the living room would do just as well for that and probably better. A chilly wind or a bit of fog always sent him inside, while my mother and I were still admiring a monarch butterfly on a frilly zinnia flower, or deploring the spittle bugs on the snow peas. Our shared enthusiasm brought us closer together than we had been since we played "Hansel and Gretel" in our garden in the hills.

Not only did we love gardens, we both loved anything to do with gardens. We liked nurseries, of course. We also loved garden supply centers and home improvement warehouses. My father couldn't understand our passion for these places. He hated those big impersonal warehouses, because when he entered a store he expected gracious surroundings, helpful clerks, and gift wrapping. My mother and I were content to wander though the enormous spaces, looking at doors, bathroom fixtures, barrels of bulbs, racks of shovels, seeds and wonderful terra cotta pots.

Our infatuation with these places was not new, only rediscovered. One of my early memories is of a manure-buying expedition with my mother. I remember driving to Sears in our old Rambler station wagon and filling the back of the car with bags of cow manure. The car was hot and the manure smelled just awful on the ride back home. That afternoon I wrote in my diary, "Mommy is in the garden spreading cow BMs on the lawn, I do not know why she is doing this, it is very stinky."

After we moved away from the big garden, my mother stopped making those trips to Sears. And even if she had kept on, I doubt I would have accompanied her. Now I found myself going again with my mother to those garden centers and filling the back of her car—a Honda, this time —with bags of cow manure.

The manure broke the ice—if that image is not too revolting to use—and finally I did what I ought to have done from the start. I stopped depending solely on books for information, and I asked my mother for help and for plants.

She gave me lots of both, showing me how to dig up her crowded perennials and divide the clumps into new plants. While she replanted smaller, rejuvenated plants, I filled big black plastic shopping bags with her leftovers. I took iris roots (rhizomes), clumps of Shasta daisies, and lots of common pink-colored yarrow (*Achillea millefolium*) with green, ferny foliage.

I didn't know the proper names of any of these gift plants and neither did my mother. She didn't even remember buying them. They had been around forever, she said. Many of them had come originally from our garden in the hills.

Those plants were special to me because they were so familiar. I especially loved the iris. I remembered those tall, purple flowers blooming every April around Eastertime. When I was a child, I thought they were the only iris in the world. Later, I was amazed to learn that the flowers come in other colors and sizes.

Now, I sat in my own backyard, breaking up the clumpy divisions of my mother's iris—cutting the rhizomes with a sharp knife, discarding the woody center, and choosing healthy sections with good fans of leaves. Suddenly I stopped and wondered, "How did I learn how to do this?" And I realized I must have paid some attention to my mother's "puttering," after all. I felt very contented, planting those iris in my garden. I felt as though a circle had been completed.

Because I hadn't planned a proper garden yet, I didn't plant the perennials in any particular order. I just dug out onion grass and clustered my freebie plants around the vegetable plot. Since then, I have moved every clump at least once.

Spacing-Out at the Back of the Classroom

Though I was slowly making myself into a gardener, I remained fundamentally a student. I enjoyed chatting with my mother in the aisles of the garden center, but I still spent a lot of time talking to students at the library about the other parts of my life. To my surprise, I discovered that I spoke a different language now.

"A six pack," to most students, contained beer, not seedlings. A "hoe" was a rude name for a girl. "Leggy" was an attractive characteristic, not a form of weak growth caused by inadequate light. And a "deadhead" was a fan of the Grateful Dead, not a dead or dying flower. These misunderstandings were minor matters of vocabulary, but I discovered more important differences, too. Our attitudes were different.

My classmates seemed oblivious to their physical surroundings—as I had been only months before. When my Irish literature professor told an Old Irish story about the summer solstice, he had to explain that the summer solstice is the longest day of the year. The other students had a very hazy idea of what he meant. But my experience was direct. When the professor said, "The summer solstice is when the sun reaches its northernmost point," I immediately thought about my garden.

That's when I'll know, I thought, if the sun will ever reach that clump of Japanese anemone I planted on the north side of the house. That's when the shadow of the acacia tree will be at its longest across the grass. After that, I'll have lived in my house from the shortest day of the year to the longest day of the year and I'll know everything I need to know about the way the sun moves in my garden.

I listened closely to what the professor said, because I felt more involved with the sun than I ever had before, as though I actually interacted with the sun, though all I really did was take from it. I learned that in Irish folklore the sun represents the sacred king of the year, and that on the solstice the sun-king travels to an island in the north, and dies. After that night, a new king takes over as the earth goddess' consort, as the sun heads south again.

After I heard that story, I always noticed the position of the sunset. The king is heading north, I thought, as the months passed and the position moved from Foster City in the south up to San Francisco. For one glorious week, it set right over the Golden Gate bridge. Then it headed north to Marin county. The king died somewhere around San Rafael, I believe.

All that semester, when my body was in the classroom, my mind was in the garden. And, surprisingly, the reverse was also true. It was a confusing but worthwhile experience to live two lives at once. I was surprised to find that much of what I learned as a gardener made me a more sensitive student. Though my passion for gardening did not bring me closer to the other students, it did enrich my studies. One body of knowledge enhanced the other.

Chapter Two
That Awkward Age

The Greedy Gardener

I decided to wait until I graduated from college in May to start designing a real garden. In the meantime, I focused on tidying the front yard and tending the vegetable patch in the back. The vegetables, in particular, occupied me.

Although I hated to cook, I found that I really liked to grow food. I liked going out to the garden to pick lettuce, carrots, snow peas, and Johnny Jump Ups for a springtime salad. I especially loved tromping back into the kitchen, all muddy and outdoorsy, and plunking down the bowl of produce on the counter where Paul was mixing salad dressing. My primitive satisfaction at these times was so great, I could almost have grunted, "ME GROW FOOD!"

I harvested calla lilies, too, throughout the spring. A dozen of the elegant white flowers usually decorated our kitchen table, while another dozen stood on the mantel. I picked the calla lilies because they made good cut flowers —and to be perfectly honest, I picked them because I knew I could never have afforded to buy them from a florist. Whenever I passed a flower stand, I glanced at the buckets of calla lilies and thought to myself, "A buck each! My god. I've got dozens at home."

The Fuchsia Border

Tidying the front yard was less immediately satisfying. I pulled weeds, chopped weeds, dug up weeds, and made an effort to care for the few nonweedy plants that grew there. Besides a flood of calla lilies, there was the neglected fuchsia—a venerable old thing, with a twisted, peeling trunk as thick as my arm. Nothing grew near that lone fuchsia except Bermuda grass and wild violets. For quite a while I puzzled over what to plant with it.

Finally, I decided, "Fuchsias go well with fuchsias." So I took a stroll around the neighborhood with my clippers in hand and gathered three more varieties. In jars of water on the window sill, they soon sprouted roots. When I planted them in the garden, the cuttings grew as big as the original shrub, forming a colorful hedge. Eventually, they grew high enough to partly obscure the front window. Anyone sitting inside on the sofa could look out at the dangling blossoms and often at the darting hummingbirds that fed on their nectar.

Though the shrubs were a success, for a while they stood alone, because I couldn't decide what to plant beneath them. I found the shaggy, bulky plants, dripping with unsubtle color difficult to combine with other perennials.

First I tried Shasta daisies—simply because I had some divisions lying around. That was a big mistake, for the daisies quickly became as bushy as the fuchsias. Together, they were a picture of disorder.

Then I replaced the Shasta daisies with pools of sea thrift (*Armeria maritima*). In early spring, the thrift raised magenta pom-poms that perfectly matched the pinkish-purple fuchsias. For a while, I was satisfied.

Sculpting Trees

Despite the distractions of the vegetable patch and the front yard, I grew restless by spring break. I still had not done much to the back yard. I wanted to improve the space in some quick, dramatic way, so I decided to convert the lemon bush and quince shrub back into trees. I was too inexperienced to know that spring is a bad time to prune. Since then, I've learned not to prune when leaves are growing or falling. Luckily, the much-abused trees were tough enough to survive one more offense against them.

And they did need cutting. They were dense, congested things, with about ten trunks each. Some of the extra trunks had to stay, since they were fused together at the bottom, but most of them could go. The question was, which ones? Before I could start sawing, I had to find the trees within the tangles.

After a little reflection, I reduced the quince to a fan of four graceful trunks. The lemon bush, however, was more difficult to prune. I knew that no matter how I cut it, it would never look remotely like a normal tree. In the end, I went for a dramatic look, and kept three especially sinuous trunks, which twisted and curved like belly dancers' arms.

New shoots sprouted from the old cut-away trunks almost at once, as the trees tried to revert to shrubs. A few snips of the clippers from time to time took care of that problem.

Today—years later—the results of that first excavation still please me. I have concealed the thick, misshapen bases of the trees in drifts of *Crocosmia masoniorum*, effectively hiding their shrubby past. In fact, they look almost graceful now. They also take up less space in the border and cast less shadow over the ground. And between them, they obligingly hold up a hammock.

The Next Step

The next step, unfortunately, was not something Paul and I could do ourselves. We decided to hire professionals to tear down the rotting garage and remove the monstrous acacia tree. It was the only time we ever paid for help.

We were glad to have the work done. When the garage came down, the back yard grew a third larger, and with the acacia tree gone, the whole space was sunnier. The pepper tree was so happy to have the acacia out of the way, that it put out a flourish of ferny green leaves and quickly doubled in size.

Non-Sexist Soil Improvement

During that last semester of college I didn't have much time to work in the garden, but I managed to think about it a lot. I made mental lists of what I would do when I graduated.

At the top of the lists was always, "Improve the soil!" I knew I had to amend the dirt in my garden before I could begin to plant in earnest. The soil was nutrient-rich, but heavy—gummy in winter, hard and cracked in summer.

The project intimidated me a little. The garden writers I read were always bragging about how many tons of manure or compost or peat moss they had "incorporated" into their soil before planting. That word, "incorporated," struck me as a good one. It made me wonder exactly how the incorporating was done. Was it with a plow? A rototiller? Or with someone else's arms and back? Where did these gardeners get all that incorporatable stuff? And how much did it cost?

Still, I was anxious to follow the recommendations of other gardeners and incorporate my share of soil amendments into my back yard. So in late spring, as my birthday neared, I hinted that a truckload of mushroom compost or chicken manure would make a really wonderful gift. When the day arrived, I listened for the sound of a dump truck backing into the driveway. The truck never came. My family had laughed away my request for birthday compost: they thought I was joking.

Worried, I wondered how I could plant my garden without having "incorporated" anything into it. Then I read a book that convinced me that I did not need to dig all that compost into to my soil, after all.

The book was the Ruth Stout classic, the *No-Work Garden Book*. I found a worn paperback on a shelf in my parents' garage. The first chapter was called, "Throw Away Your Spade and Hoe!" I liked that very much, since I didn't own a spade or a hoe. I felt less inadequate after I read that chapter.

The whole book was about the wonders of mulch. Cover everything with mulch, it said. Mulch represses weeds, conserves water, and most of all improves the texture of the soil. If you mulch long enough you won't even need a shovel. The ground will be so soft you'll be able to plant a tree with your bare hands.

Wonderful.

Of course the information was not exactly new. In fact, that old paperback was left over from my parents' hippie veggie-garden phase, when they raised chickens and lugged bales of hay home from the country to tuck around their tomatoes and "cukes."

It was news to me, however, and I took it to heart. From the very beginning, I mulched. Not with eight inches of material, as Ruth Stout recommended. But with whatever I could scrounge up. My own garden didn't yield enough clippings for mulch, so I began to snitch bags of lawn trimmings from the curbs around the neighborhood.

Unlike Ruth Stout, I also kept compost piles. I couldn't quite bring myself to let weeds and orange peels and coffee grounds and plant clippings rot right in the beds. After all, I wanted the garden to look pretty. Besides, I had read elsewhere that plant debris left in beds breeds fungi and slugs and diseases. "Clean out your beds!" those books insisted, "Sweep and rake and cultivate!"

Those persnickety disease-conscious authors almost convinced me to clear out all my mulch. Then I realized they wanted me to pick every leaf out of the beds, only to cover the ground again with bags of store-bought mulch. That seemed silly. So I compromised. I tossed all my weeds and clippings and kitchen scraps into the compost, and mulched neatly, using leaves, grass, and properly rotted homemade compost.

For compost-making, I put aside Ruth Stout and consulted a special compost manual. It instructed me to pile the materials in tiers like a layer cake, and to carefully maintain the balance between carbon and nitrogen and between moisture and dryness. It even declared, in rather breathless prose, that if I created a good, hot compost pile I would be able to rot a slaughtered calf in half a week without producing an odor that might offend the neighbors.

The loads of technical information within the covers of that slim compost manual paralyzed me for a while. I was not sure I could construct the sophisticated compost piles it described. Eventually, I gave the booklet away to a friend and decided to compost in my own low-key way, in one of those spinning barrel composters.

I still have that composter. I like it because it's neat and small. Sometimes, however, I find myself with extra debris. When that happens—usually in the fall—I pile the surplus somewhere in the side yard, near the acanthus, and forget about it until spring. In the meantime, mice make nests in it, birds steal twigs from it, and I suppose a lot of nutrients leach out. Eventually, though, the weeds resolve themselves into credible compost, so that sometime in March I usually enjoy a day of frenzied compost spreading.

My experience with the compost manual proved to me that I wasn't very good at following instructions in books. I did stick with Ruth Stout pretty closely, though. And I followed one piece of her advice to the letter. I never "dug in" and I never rototilled.

My aversion to rototillers began long before I had a garden of my own, on the day that I helped my father-in-law prepare the soil for his vegetable garden. The machine my father-in-law rented was noisy and exhausting to use. It was expensive to rent and would have been even more expensive to buy. But most of all, that rototiller seemed like bad news to me because it was violent.

I still feel the same way about those machines. Maybe it's my old hippie heritage breaking out, but I don't like the way rototillers tear up the ground. I think of that old cliche of the plow being the man and the earth being the woman and the man being active and the woman being passive and the man splitting open and the woman receiving, and the whole image seems too pseudoreligious and primitive to me.

More importantly, however, rototillers besides being distasteful are not even necessary. The blades loosen the top few of inches of soil, and then create a hardpan further down. And they chop up the worms, too. Not to speak of microorganisms—those invisible creatures that improve soil texture and break down soil particles and fertilizers and release plant nutrients. Most of the books and manuals I've consulted advise gardeners not to disturb the microorganisms, and what could be more disturbing than whirring steel blades?

From the very beginning, I banned rototillers from my garden.

I could, of course, have turned over the soil manually, instead. But I never did. I was almost as squeamish about digging as I was about rototilling. I didn't even like digging holes for plants, because every time I thrust a shovel into the ground I sliced up worms. I was not sure whether the worms survived this treatment or not, but the sight of those squirming halves disturbed me.

Of course, I couldn't avoid digging holes now and then. But at least I could refrain from turning over the earth. I liked the idea of the mulch slowly decomposing and improving the soil from the top down, gently.

Ruth Stout's method worked well for me. As the years passed, the ground underneath the mulch grew softer and wormier. Today, I even occasionally dig a hole with my bare hands—not to prove an ideological point, but probably because I have misplaced my trowel. Granted, they are only *small* holes at the front of the border—I have not managed tree-holes yet—but considering the ground I started with, even a small hole isn't bad.

Liberty

After graduation, I began to plant. I planted, and planted, and planted. All through May and June, flowers spread across my backyard. I didn't worry about design. I just popped the plants in the ground as I acquired them. Divisions from my mother's garden went in first. Then, I added some mail-order plants and some perennials from the nursery. Later, when the annuals I had grown from seed grew large enough to set out, I studded the ground with sturdy little French marigolds, and sweet alyssum.

"Look at my flowers," I said. It didn't occur to me to say, "Look at my garden." I still had no thought of an over-all scheme.

But I did have a lot of fun. Gardening seemed ridiculously easy at that stage. Every change felt like a step forward, a stride away from a weed meadow toward a flowery haven.

Panic in the Garden

Unfortunately, that stage of giddy progress did not last. As spring passed into summer, I began to sense that something was wrong, and slowly my uneasiness grew. Maybe I had more time to notice the garden's flaws now that I was out of school. Or maybe the flaws were more glaring because the plantings had at last begun to mature.

As the summer-flowering perennials burst into lusty bloom, unfortunate color combinations cropped up everywhere. (In particular, I remember a sun-yellow coreopsis blooming next to a bubble-gum pink pelargonium. The bright crepe paper-colors might have looked cheerful on a Mexican pinata, but they were garish in my garden.) Dead plants left large, troubling gaps in some places. Other areas already seemed crowded. My garden was as awkward and homely as a student in junior high school.

Probably, some adolescent awkwardness was inevitable: every new garden goes through a difficult stage. But in my own case, inexperience added to the chaos. The problem was I had fallen in love with gardening; that did not mean, however, that I was good at it. For those first few months, I hadn't realized how badly I was doing because the simple act of growing plants had thrilled me. Now I saw that my raw enthusiasm was getting me into trouble.

I seemed to be incapable of turning down free plants. And since I adored growing flowers from seed, I grew a lot of them, in a lot of different colors. I tried to do too much in a small space. The result was bright, exuberant, life-loving —and ultimately ugly.

Of course, I was upset when I realized this. I was confused, too. I didn't understand that a successful garden depends on structure and color schemes. I still thought love and hard work were all I needed to make my garden beautiful. And so I couldn't figure out why my garden looked worse than other gardens on the block. I put so much more time and effort into my garden than other people put into theirs. Why did the yard with the clipped shrubs and neat ribbon of mums look more professional, more adult, somehow?

I felt silly—as though I were playing around, making mudpies, fingerpainting. What I was doing, really, was learning.

Floury Borders

So what did I do? Naturally, being the kind of person I was, I ran to a bookstore. This time I stayed away from plant encyclopedias and booklets full of the scientific tidbits I loved so much, and looked at books on garden design instead. I studied the gorgeous photographs and asked myself what the gardens in those books had that mine lacked.

The answer was obvious. They had defined borders, not just a rash of plants covering the ground. "I need borders," I said.

I wanted to be very professional and organized about the project so I went from the bookstore straight to the stationary store, where I bought a pad of graph paper. At home that night I sat at the kitchen table covering page after page with my plans.

Although I certainly enjoyed myself, after a while I had to admit that I didn't know what I was doing. The plans on paper simply did not seem real to me; I suspected that they wouldn't seem real until I transferred them to the earth itself. I had to see the lines on the ground. I had to pace along the shapes of the borders and stand inside of them.

So the next day I drew the designs all over again. But this time, instead of using pencil on paper, I sprinkled flour out of a bag, drawing the borders right on the ground.

This method was more satisfactory. Even then, though, I couldn't decide right away how to shape the borders. For one thing, I wasn't sure if I wanted curves or straight lines. I tried curves first, because I remembered reading that they are more naturalistic than straight lines. But how curvy is curvy? The first line I drew, as fluted as a pie crust, clearly would not do. So I squirted the flour away with the hose and tried again.

The second time, I drew a gently curving line. It looked much better. I drew another line and then another. And feeling inspired at last, I dashed across the ground with the flour bag under my arm and a wooden scoop in my hand, casting down more lines, shaping the garden. Flour flew everywhere. When I was finished, a fine, powdery mist hung over the yard.

For a month or so, my borders pleased me. Then gradually, I became aware that I had made them too small. Like many unimaginative new gardeners, I had followed the perimeters of the fence, ringing the yard with narrow planting areas, and leaving too much empty space in the middle of the yard. I knew I needed to put flower beds, a tree or two, grass, and maybe a patio in the middle of the yard. But the space intimidated me. I could plant a vegetable plot there, knowing it would be temporary. I hesitated, however, to position permanent features in the middle of the empty yard.

Today, the back yard looks very different. I've added beds and enlarged the borders I first drew in flour, years ago. Nonetheless, I made a start that morning: I began at least to try to organize my garden.

Looking for Rules

It's hard to describe just how bewildered I felt that summer. It wasn't an easy time. I often found myself looking back nostalgically to those spring days when everything I had done in my garden had seemed magically right.

Now, nothing I did seemed right. So I returned to the bookstore and studied the photographs again.

"I've got borders," I thought. "What do I need to do now?"

This time, I noticed that the gardens in the pictures all included lots of tall plants in their designs. My own back yard, with its groups of short, immature perennials and short, bright annuals, looked as though I had taken a buzz saw and given it a crewcut.

I thought maybe I needed to break up my level borders with some tall plants. And then, as I read a little of the text below the pictures, I became even more certain that this should be my next step.

"All gardens benefit from tall plants," the book said. "Even mature gardens need vertical accents to break up the rounded, billowing plants that dominate most borders. Vertical accents are always welcome and difficult to overuse."

So the book said. I, however, managed to do the almost-impossible. (Call it beginner's luck in reverse.) I planted an absolutely overwhelming stand of Siberian iris in the middle of the back border.

I could tell that the iris were too strong for the spot almost before they had recovered from transplant shock. Whenever I looked out the kitchen window, those five-foot-tall blades — like a barricade in the middle of the border— stopped my eye and drew my gaze up, away from the rest of the plants.

I had sandwiched the iris between daylilies (*Hemerocallis*), hoping that those fainting swords would ease the eye downward away from the iris, and into the rest of the garden. But the plan failed: the iris were too forceful. They were all that I saw. Next to them, the daylilies were absolutely insignificant.

"And yet, the plan looks fine on paper," I said, showing my sketch to Paul. In the drawing, the iris seemed to be just what I needed to create a sense of enclosure around the back of the border. I didn't understand.

(Later, I realized that my plans always looked fine on paper, the drawings invariably tidy and convincing. But those neat little cloud-shaped "drifts" and "masses" drawn on graph paper often hid terrible mistakes.)

I lived with that tall, broad screen of foliage for two weeks. Finally, I couldn't stand it. I set out with my shovel one morning and dug them all up. I knew they had to go. But how did I know? What did I see in the garden that I had been unable to perceive on paper?

Years later, I still wonder what makes a border "just right"—as Goldilocks would say. Why does a large drift of a single perennial sometimes look peaceful and sometimes seem dull? Why does a mixed planting of several kinds of plants sometimes seem exciting and sometimes look chaotic?

Is it the color scheme? The size of the drifts? The density of the planting?

I'm not sure. I only know that if I tinker around with a design long enough, it eventually pleases me. At least for a time.

A Matter of Taste

That summer, out of college, I spent hours studying the instructions in plant books. I was searching for codes that would tell me: This works, that doesn't work; this is good, that is ugly.

Gradually, I came to accept that I would never find rules I could trust. For one thing, the expert gardeners all seemed to contradict each other. Even my mother and I couldn't agree. I was always discovering that some feature in my garden that I found particularly lovely, looked unlovely to her.

She visited once toward the end of that summer, when the garden was full of bloom. Along the front walk, some tall, white daisies (*Boltonia asteroides* 'Snowbank') thrust through a stand of pale pink Japanese anemone (*Anemone japonica*). I had dug the anemones out of my mother's garden, but the boltonia was from a nursery. The flower was my own discovery, and I was proud of it. Because it was a breezy day, the anemone rustled a bit and the boltonia bowed forward and backward across the walkway. The disorder, however, didn't bother me. I thought the flowers looked charming, in a wild, cottagey sort of way.

But my mother thrust the leaning flowers out of her way and looked scathingly at them as she passed. "Now you see why I don't grow those, the way they flop."

I remembered that moment often as I worked on my garden that first, difficult year. Whenever I got too bogged down trying to analyze exactly what I was doing and why I was doing it, whenever I stopped and searched for a rule or a law that would tell me whether what I was doing was right, I usually ended up shrugging and telling myself, "Who knows why? I'm doing this because I like it this way."

Intuition

I tried to be a less cerebral gardener, depending less on books and more on good sense. I did not, however, give up trying to impose some structure on my chaotic back yard. I went about it differently, though. Instead of working out a design on paper (as I had with those sadly inappropriate iris) I learned to look at the garden itself. I spent a lot of time that summer staring at and brooding over troublesome spots in the garden, trying to figure out why they bothered me.

I usually worked at a problem for a while in the same way that I would tug on a stubborn dandelion root. And like a root finally popping out, the answers often came suddenly.

For weeks, I searched fruitlessly for a way to improve the north side of the front yard, near the bedroom window. Then, on my way in from a walk one afternoon, the solution came to me. Ferns!

The problem was that the dusty millers (*Senecio cineraria* 'Silver Dust') had outgrown their positions. Sometime during the year, they had turned into huge, shapeless monsters —felted grey on the outside, sodden brown on the inside— home to dozens of similarly monstrous snails. The Shasta daisies next to the dusty millers had grown floppy and shapeless, too.

"I need nice vertical ferns," I thought again, and immediately I started digging everything up. The massive dusty millers went into the compost, where they refused to decompose. I transplanted the Shasta daisies to a spot where they could flop happily. Then I dug up some ferns growing wild on the side of the house. I also fetched two *Gaura lindheimeri* that had become overcrowded in their pots. I mixed some compost into the holes, plunked in the plants and watered them well. Then I went inside the house and tried to remember what I should have been doing after my walk instead of gardening.

When I woke the next morning, I wondered what had I done. In the frenzy of digging plants and hauling buckets of water and compost, I had stopped thinking rationally. I had become a gardening animal—all hard shoulder muscles and sensitive fingertips.

I ran outside in my nightgown to look at the front yard, to see what I had created in my frenzy. I was relieved. The ferns were listing somewhat, but in general, the planting looked fine.

I had been foolish to worry, really. Since that day, I have decided that when I obey my impulses the changes usually *do* look fine. The gardening animal is an inspired creature, and inspired creatures rarely make mistakes.

Changes

That summer, I learned to respect my instincts. But I also came to realize that sometimes the garden itself makes the rules. To a certain extent, it imposes its own order, improving itself almost independently of me.

My experience with the border along the driveway is a good example of the way in which the garden helped to create itself. The border is a narrow, sunny, dry one—what garden writer Penelope Hobhouse would call a ribbon border. I visualized daisies there, lots of daisies. Big white Shasta daisies, small white marguerites, yellow coreopsis (*Coreopsis grandiflora* 'Early Sunrise.') And something blue.

I set off to the nursery looking for blue daisies, and came home with felicia and asters. The asters—beloved by gardeners in the northeast—hardly lived long enough to die. But the tender felicia (*Felicia amelloides*), grown as an annual in colder climates, thrived in my garden for years.

I emphasized the felicia's yellow eyes by planting it beside the coreopsis, creating what Pamela J. Harper would call a "color echo." The big yellow daises and the little blue yellow-eyed daisies grew beautifully in that hot border.

Then, in an act of witlessness that embarrasses me now, I put *Ligularia*, 'The Rocket,' behind the daisies. I believe that the point of this dreadful combination was for the yellow ligularia to add height and verticality to the daisy border.

Of course, I couldn't begin to water the ligularia enough. The plant belongs in a bog! At first I tried to keep it wet, but soon I gave up. All through August, its gorgeous jagged leaves lay limply on the soil, condemning me. Pretty soon I hated to go near it. I began avoiding the driveway. Eventually, the poor ligularia died, and I replaced it with a few surprisingly unthirsty yellow perennial foxgloves (*Digitalis ambigua*).

After that, when I looked at the border—ligularia-less, aster-less, but crowded with daisies and foxgloves—I asked myself, "Did I design this or did the garden design it?"

I learned to admit that my six-foot wooden fence encloses a living thing. The different parts of the garden grow and die and subtly adjust themselves as the seasons go by, with or without my intervention.

The Wrong Plants

I discovered that some of my favorite plants languished in the Bay Area's climate. Perhaps my greatest disappointment was my inability to grow lupines. Years ago in Brittany, I had admired masses of lupines growing in marvelously un-French cottage gardens. I loved the way the tall flowers stood up like electrocuted wisteria. I coveted those lupines. I lusted after them.

But eventually, I gave up on them. After replacing my wretched clump twice that first year, I took a hint from the other plants in the back yard. Next to the deceased lupines, some *Salvia greggii* and lantana were living happy lives. I had to admit that even if the lupines had survived, they would have seemed out of place among those water-thrifty plants. The fact is, the lupines *were* out of place.

That autumn, I also planted delphiniums in the back yard. I was inspired, I suppose, by dreamy photographs of blue spires touching blue skies. Come to think of it, I had never seen a real delphinium in a real garden. Yet I believed fervently that a garden without delphiniums was not a garden worth having.

The following spring, in the back of the border, the plants raised sickly seven-inch blooms half-hidden by the bearded iris in front. Anyone fond of stately blue delphiniums winced at the ones in my garden.

Why did they fail to grow? Because I didn't water them enough or give them the rich diet they deserved.

I handled my plants with a sort of "tough love." Instead of digging in pounds and pounds of manure when I set the plants in the ground, I threw in a handful or two of compost and backfilled the cavity mostly with old soil. I was afraid that if I filled the hole with soil amendments, the roots would go into shock when they grew out of their small cushy environment into the real dirt. Better to work on improving the entire garden, I believed, and not just the soil in one hole.

This method worked well for lean, rugged plants such as *Salvia greggii* or lavender or coreopsis. I found out, however, during my brief and rather miserable infatuation with aristocratic border plants, that you simply will not get ten foot tall delphiniums with this system. Today, Russian sage (*Perovskia atriplicifolia*) colonizes the spot where those delphiniums once pined.

The Second Winter

Summer was bad enough, but that winter was heartbreaking. I hate to think how many plants I killed. Greedy snails accounted for some of the losses, but many plants perished simply because they could not thrive in the conditions I provided.

I was arrogant enough to believe that I could grow anything in my garden. After all, California is famous for its hospitable climate, isn't it?

But I learned an expensive lesson that year: although I can draw from a wide range of plants for my garden, that range does not include tropicals or plants that need a good winter chill.

That winter, a lovely peach hibiscus died because it froze and a lilac bush died because it did not freeze enough. I tried covering the hibiscus with a cardboard box to keep it warm on cold nights and I packed ice cubes around the lilac, but these efforts were not sufficient.

Death

I discovered that nature can be harsh even in California. Plants died, and I could do nothing about it. Bugs and rain (or lack of rain) and wind and sun and snails and more bugs and idiosyncratic plants and cats with big bladders and people with big feet all helped transform my garden. Perhaps these accidental deaths shaped it even more than I did, with all my planting and replanting.

When nature edited my garden, the change was sometimes traumatic. For instance, during that second, unusually wet, winter, my white oleander (*Nerium oleander*) died—and a lot of time and effort went with it when it passed away. I had carefully trained the shrub into a standard form. It was my first effort at topiary. The oleander stood in the back yard like a miniature tree, shading a patch of alpine strawberries and *geranium* 'Wargave Pink.'

After I removed the dead tree, a circle of ground about four feet wide opened up—a significant space in such a small garden. The area looked different without the oleander there. The mingling strawberries and geraniums no longer looked charming, but rather jumbled and haphazard.

Since I had to do something, the tragedy, in a way, turned into an opportunity. The garden had changed, again—not necessarily for better, or for worse. It had simply changed.

Birth

Over and over, nature altered the design of my garden by slaughtering my plants, but it also contributed to the landscape by adding a few plants of its own choosing. About a month after I dragged the poor dead oleander out of the soggy earth, I noticed a holly seedling about six inches tall growing near the back fence. I dug it up and put it in a pot, pleased to have received a gift from nowhere. In about a year it grew into a nice glossy dark green shrub.

Sometimes nature gave too much. When a California poppies seeded themselves in every bed and border in the entire garden, when the neighbor's red valerian (*Centranthus ruber*) sprang up in the middle of my Shasta daisies, when the nasturtiums grew up the quince tree and sweet William (*Dianthus barbatus*) popped up in a crack in the picnic table, I thought to myself, "Nature is generous but nature is also a slob."

Sometimes I rejected its gifts. I ripped out poppies in armloads. But I dribbled fertilizer over that determined little dianthus. And I decided that the red valerian made a nice accent among the white daisies. Over the years, as I made my garden, I sometimes let go. Here and there, I let the garden plant itself.

A Gardener

That December—after a whole year of trying to make a garden out of my neglected yard—I began to understand the truth about gardeners. We are complex creatures. We are contradictory.

For instance, how do we treat nature? How do we, as gardeners, interact with the natural world? We spend a lot of our time with dirt on our faces and plants in our hands. We work with the earth constantly, but how do we actually treat it? Are we active or passive? Controlling or compliant? To what extent do we shape our environment and to what extent do we let it shape itself?

Are we fussbudgets, tweaking off every deadhead and meticulously edging our lawns? Are we decadent aesthetes, working out fantastically complex combinations of texture on texture, leaf on leaf?

Or are we actually placid nature lovers infatuated with the cycles of life and death, content to watch impassively as time rolls round from spring to winter, smiling tolerantly as our seedlings grow up, blossom, and fade into compost fodder?

Are we artists shaping the land? Or are we more like babysitters, tending it, watching it, helping it? Probably most of us are all of these things.

These questions still fascinated me ten years after I first began to plant my garden. The year I was pregnant, I continued to mull over them. I always returned to a paradox: although gardening seems to be mostly about controlling nature, gardeners seem to understand better than nongardeners that ultimately nature is uncontrollable. In the end, I decided it was better to give up trying to reconcile the contradictions I saw in my own gardener's soul. The complexity intrigued me, and it intrigues me still. Moreover, the tension between these contradictions enriches my gardening experience.

Sometimes I struggle fanatically against failure. Other times, I accept defeat without the slightest tussle. I set out a formal flower bed, and then disrupt the whole scheme with a perversely informal intrusion of succulents. I landscape with native shrubs, then add exotic bulbs. I seem unable to make up my mind.

My approach to pestcontrol is equally inconsistent. To a large extent, I just sit back and hope that my healthy plants will repel attacks all by themselves, without any intervention. When I notice a few coral red aphids clustered around the bud tips of the 'Iceberg' roses, and a scattering of jade green spittle bugs flecking their spit over the bearded iris leaves, I do nothing, counting on the immense variety of plants in my garden to shelter a multiplicity of beneficial insects.

On the other hand, when mites curl the leaves of my beloved fuchsias, I get my sprayer and smother those tiny pests under a good slick layer of oil.

And always, always, I stomp ferociously on every snail I can find.

My garden is all about balance, about choices. I seem to move one way and then the other, always fluctuating, always wavering. The garden itself mirrors my ambivalence. Some months, I let Russian sage and hardy geraniums billow onto the lawn. Other times, I chop the plants well back and spread an inch or two of neat mulch between the edge of the border and the newly cut grass. My idea of beauty fluctuates. Sometimes I long for a look of abundance, other times I crave clean, severe lines. Thank goodness that my garden—though small—has room enough for all my contradictory impulses.

Chapter Three
Finding the Right Plants

How to Make Traffic Island Plants Seem Glamorous

By the next spring I was a wiser gardener, willing (or mostly willing) to let the sun, rain, fog, and soil steer the direction my yard took on its journey toward becoming a real garden. I chose my plants more carefully, and as a result I made fewer mistakes.

It was just as well I had learned my lesson, for I couldn't afford to go on making mistakes. I was beginning to realize how expensive a small garden could be, especially if half the plants in the garden died before reaching maturity. Humbled by all the disasters of the previous year, I vowed that second spring to stay away from the nurseries as much as possible, planting only divisions from other people's gardens.

Of course, the plants I acquired from my friends were nothing special. They were all surplus plants, plants people did not mind giving away: agapanthus, trailing African daisies (*Osteospermum fruticosum*), crocosmia, daylilies, and gazanias. Paul called them traffic island plants.

He may have been right, but he missed the fact that the plants from my friends' gardens offered several advantages.

They were free—that was the main advantage—but besides that, they also had proven that they would flourish in the local climate. They were healthy, placid plants. Overused, underloved, easy to grow, easy to divide, quick to establish, and invulnerable to pests. Not a neurotic specimen among them.

Even so, I wasn't sure I liked having a yard full of what Paul called "banal plants." At least, at first I wasn't. But I told myself that the plants had acquired their bad reputations because people commonly misused them. I told myself that it did not matter which plants I used in my garden, so long as I used them imaginatively. "Just because most people treat a particular plant as a kind of outdoor carpeting doesn't mean I have to do the same," I said to Paul.

For example, gardeners usually plant African daisies in masses. One popular design features a thick band of purple daisies backed by another band of glittering white gravel. This is an admittedly low-maintenance scheme, but one reminiscent of gardens in front of banks or dry cleaners or gas stations. It's designed to be seen from a car—a stripe of purple and a stripe of dazzling white flashing in the corner of your eye as you drive down the street. No wonder the *Sunset Western Garden Book* calls them "a little coarse (and a bit ho-hum)."

I used African daisies differently. Instead of growing them in a mass, I allowed the individual plants to wind through the borders, filling the bare spots. Today, after nearly ten years of roaming through the garden, they pop up in some unexpected places. In one spot in the back yard, in what has become the purple border, white African daisies with purple underpetals thread among my mother's purple iris.

The juxtaposition is purely serendipitous. The only influence I had on the arrangement was to extricate the white daisies with purple undersides from the tangle of plants I dug out of my father-in-law's garden and to toss the purple daisies with white undersides into the compost pile. The purple daisies were a bit too purple, I decided. Even with free plants, it pays to be a little picky.

I was also quite choosy about the gazanias, taking only two colors from the six that grew jumbled together in my step-mother-in-law's parking strip—reds and yellows next to oranges and pinks. I selected the colors I liked, dug them up, and planted them separately. The bald spots in my step-mother-in-law's garden soon filled in, and my plugs grew quickly into round shaggy mats, ideal for the front of my garden's borders.

Several of them still grow at the front of the burgundy border, along the back yard's rear fence. In later years, I discovered that the gazania's grey-green foliage mixes well with lamb's ears (*Stachys lanata*). I particularly like a combination of lamb's ears and mahogany-red gazanias growing in front of a spray of purple fountain grass (*Pennisetum setaceum* 'Rubrum') and a hillock of grey licorice plant (*Helichrysum*).

When I planted my freebie plants that second spring, I was not yet very experienced at combining plants in interesting ways. But I did have good luck with agapanthus—which is surprising, because I had a hard time persuading Paul to let agapanthus into our garden at all. He hated the plant. But I convinced him that he was prejudiced against it because he seldom had seen it growing in groups of less than fifty. He had seen masses of agapanthus growing in front of a mortuary. He had seen masses of them outside of McDonald's. And he had seen them in my mother's garden, edging the driveway.

"They aren't so bad," I insisted.

My mother was not encouraging. "They're snail hotels," she said. "However, if you want them, help yourself. Take dozens. I won't miss them."

So I divided a few clumps. But instead of lining them up in long rows, I planted them here and there beneath the lemon tree, with daylilies. Then I fetched Paul and showed him how well the bold, dark, straplike agapanthus leaves mixed with the paler, thinner, more delicate leaves of the daylily. Paul could not have cared less about the foliage, but when summer came he *did* see the beauty of the blue globes of the agapanthus and the daylilies' rust-orange trumpets rising above the green clumps of leaves.

Paul's sister's garden provided another free plant: crocosmia. Not the fancy red 'Lucifer,' but the old-fashioned orange variety, which grew like weeds around her garage. I dug them up and plunked a shovelful into a hole behind the agapanthus and daylilies. The crocosmia shoved in everywhere but found the other plants as tough and nearly as invasive in return. I let them fight their own fight, and in August sat back and enjoyed the orange dragonfly flowers.

In the front, I added spider plants (*Chlorophytum comosum*) rooted from my mother-in-law's house plants. Then, I looked around and tried to see what other free plants I could come up with. My own garden offered an endless supply of calla lilies, but at first, I didn't want to use them. I disliked calla lilies almost as much as Paul disliked agapanthus. Though I admired the flowers in bouquets, I thought the plants were overused in foundation planting all over the Bay Area.

The problem with calla lilies, I decided, is that they never want to stay in small groups. A few plants arching from a narrow base are graceful and lovely. But when the base widens, and the silhouette grows square or rectangular instead of triangular, the effect is overpowering.

Not only had most of my clumps spread too wide, the individual plants had grown too large. Some were five feet tall, with stems thicker than my thumb. They were simply too big. After I figured that out, I gave away all the potato-sized tubers and kept the small ones, which sent out delicate stems and elegant flowers.

The calla lilies joined my array of "banal plants," and even enhanced the arrangement. The calla lilies' leaves, like dark glossy tongues, stuck out boldly through the clumps of agapanthus, daylilies, and spider plant.

I made a sort of set piece out my collection of scorned plants and repeated the arrangement in several places in the back yard. True, when people visited me that second summer, they didn't exactly flop down on their knees and swear that I had opened their eyes afresh to the sinuous beauty of African daisies. I have to admit, in fact, that most people didn't even notice the "common" plants mixed in with more unusual ones. But that was fine with me. I decided that as long as people responded to the atmosphere of the garden, I didn't expect them to notice the individual plants.

Growing Up, Growing Upward

After my unfortunate experience with the imposing Siberian iris, I had hesitated to add more major vertical accents to the back yard, choosing, instead, to plant clumps of smaller, spiky perennials. These standard, dependable accents, mostly consisted of clumps of bearded iris and clumps of crocosmia, along with a few clumps of ferns. These well-used devices, though they helped to break up expanses of short bushy perennials (such as coreopsis and lavender) and short husky annuals (including French marigolds and calendula), did not seem to be strong enough. So at planting time, that second fall, I decided to be bold and insert a few solitary specimens into the back yard, instead of adding more clumps of pointy plants.

For a powerful accent, I chose Mediterranean fan palm (*Chamaerops*). This palm is very slow-growing, drought-resistant, and tough enough to stand a light frost. It's also a splendidly sculptural plant. It looks wonderful striking out dramatically above a carpet of small succulents and sedums.

That autumn I also searched for a slightly more relaxed accent to use in the borders and I came up with *Asparagus meyeri*. This ornamental asparagus is a friendly plant, with fuzzy fern-green foliage like bunches of racoon tails. It looks especially cheerful wagging behind bright *Lantana* 'Confetti.'

The fronts of the borders needed vertical emphasis, too, I realized. After casting around for a while, I remembered the *Aloe nobilis* growing in my mother's desert garden. Though aloe is short—only about eight inches high—it's unquestionably a vertical plant. After a little persuasion, my mother parted with a few divisions, which transplanted easily, even without roots. I used the toothy, dark green succulent to break up expanses of candytuft (*Iberis* 'Purity'), spider plant, miniature agapanthus, and other edging plants.

Foliage plants are, of course, the easiest vertical accents to use in a border, but I also tried to mix in some tall flowers for height. I found annuals especially useful, since they bloom steadily throughout their short lives. Tall, ferny cosmos quickly became one of my favorites.

Biennials seemed less useful as vertical accents. As Paul said, "They sit around for a year before blooming and then die as soon as they do." That year I planted hollyhocks and foxgloves, but I thought of them as Loch Ness monsters (lovely Loch Ness monsters), rearing their heads at the back of the borders for a few weeks in May. I didn't expect them to do anything more than surprise me with their fleeting magic.

Flowering perennials seemed slightly more useful than the biennials. Unfortunately, I had already discovered that many of them flower for only a few weeks each year. Oriental poppies (*Papaver orientale*), for instance, lift their flowers as much as five feet high, but die down again in two or three weeks.

Wanting something more long lasting, I searched that autumn for tall, fall-blooming perennials that would be in flower for a month or more. I came home with four-inch pots of *Liatris spicata* 'Kobold', and obedient plants (*Physostegia virginiana*). They turned out to be wonderfully spiky flowers, as vertical accents ought to be. Unfortunately, they weren't exactly the vertical accents I was looking for, since I couldn't depend on them to contribute structure to the winter garden.

Learning to Use Unsociable Perennials

My search for vertical accents that second year taught me a lot about perennials: for one thing, all perennials change shape throughout the year, but tall ones do so sensationally. The drama of these transformations drew my attention to the nature of herbaceous perennials in general.

Almost all of them, short, tall and in between—from penstemon and Russian sage, to coreopsis, yarrow and veronica—and scores of others, are negligible lumps most of the year. In my garden, they don't die down in winter, but become even more negligible and lumpish. When they bloom, they explode into unruly masses of flowers. Their yearly caterpillar-to-butterfly-and-back-again transformation makes them difficult to use well.

That year, I learned to plan in reverse, asking myself, "When this perennial bursts into bloom, will it mess up the overall scheme?" rather than "Will it help?"

Hollyhock mallow (*Malva alcea* 'Fastigiata') is a perfect example of a charming, maddening perennial. I love its sprays of small pale pink blossoms, but the flowers only last two weeks. The rest of the plant remains in the border all year—and it is not especially pretty.

That autumn, I planted hollyhock mallow in several different spots. The following year, I walked around the garden noting which plantings were successes and which were disappointments. The experience taught me a lot, though mostly through failure.

I paired the mallow with daylilies, but the daylilies grew larger than I anticipated, smothering the more delicate plants around it. The unlucky mallow bloomed in a fountain of daylily foliage.

In the back yard, where the white oleander once stood, I tried mallow behind the drift of alpine strawberries and *Geranium* 'Wargave Pink.' I imagined the pink flowers mingling gorgeously, but the geranium bloomed in April and the mallow flowered four months later, so that combination failed, too.

In the front yard, I managed to pull off a mild success. I paired the mallow with Russian sage. In August, the sage's blue pipe-cleaner flowers waved among the mallow's delicate pink spires. The alliance was pretty enough, if not dramatic. I knew, however, that in winter, both plants would hunker down unsociably, leaving me with nothing to admire.

As a result, I decided I could not afford to let the combination remain in such a conspicuous part of the front yard.

I realized that I shouldn't have attempted to mix the mallow with other perennials. The less acrobatic companions were more dependable. I found shrubby cape mallow (*Anisodontea capensis*) especially effective. Of all the combinations I tried that year, this pairing of the cape and the hollyhock mallows is the only one that remains in my garden today.

The shrubby plant definitely rules, flowering from April until October, and keeping its fanlike shape even in winter. When the hollyhock mallow blooms in August, its pink disk-shaped flowers and upright shape enhance the shrub's good looks, but it does little more than add a second—temporary—layer of beauty to the part of the border already dominated by the shrub.

This discovery strengthened my bias against herbaceous perennials. I already had learned to do without the peonies, delphiniums, lupines, astilbes, and asters of East Coast and English gardens. Now I was also starting to turn away from the drought-resistant perennials popular in other West Coast gardens. After all, an out-of-bloom penstemon is just as dull as an out of bloom delphinium.

I was starting to prefer shrubby plants. Defining these preferences took me a long way toward creating the garden I truly wanted. All my experimentation those second and third years—messing around with annuals, perennials and shrubs—taught me a lot about the way different plants behave.

Plotting the Third Year

By the third year, fewer plants were dying in my garden. I had more skill in keeping plants alive, or at least I had more skill in choosing plants that kept themselves alive. I was also starting to realize that making a garden is about more than just raising plants. I didn't want to choose plants based solely on the fact that I could keep them alive. So what did I want?

Strangely enough, I had never considered the question before. During that third winter, I tried to find the answer. One warm day in January, when Paul and I were picnicking on the lawn, it came to me.

"I want the garden to be a place we can spend time in all year long," I decided. "I want to live in it. I want to eat breakfast, read, talk with friends, take a nap, balance the checkbook, look at the mail, eat lunch, write letters, play with my niece and her border collie, eat dinner, daydream, be romantic, be silly, be sociable, be alone."

And I wanted to do all this throughout the year.

Once I had figured out what I wanted from my garden, I understood more clearly how to plant it.

I knew that if I expected my garden to look attractive all year, I couldn't let an abundance of bloom in June mean bare ground in January. After all, June often marks the start of the Bay Area's fog season, while January can be warm. I wanted the garden to look pretty all year, just in case I decided to have a barbecue on New Year's Day or a Halloween garden party.

So once more, the perennials were the losers. In a different climate, I might not have minded a garden full of perennials. In my California garden, however, there *is* no out-of-season time when out-of-season plants are acceptable. It's foolish to select perennials that feel the four seasons in their bones (or in their stems) only to plant them in a part of the country where the seasons are much more mixed up than that.

When I looked around my garden at the start of the third year, I discovered a funny thing. The acanthus, agapanthus, African daisies, and gazanias—the easy-to-care-for plants, the freebie plants, the tender plants that flourish without any help from me—all looked pretty much in January as they had looked in July.

I resolved to use more evergreen plants with shapely foliage, more shrubs, more ferns, more grasses, more succulents, even more "parking strip" plants, and to plant fewer of the customary perennials, or at least to use those perennials sparingly, as accents. I became interested in trying to recreate the classic borders I saw in books, using my own blend of sturdy, well-loved plants.

Every Inch Counts

As a beginning gardener, I had looked around my small back yard and asked myself questions such as, "Where can I put my river of grape hyacinths? Where should the rose bed be? Where would a swath of heather look most beautiful?"

Once I had defined a year-round garden as my goal, though, I surrendered some of the more fanciful ideas lifted from glossy gardening books. I realized that such extravagant, one-season planting schemes would have to wait until I had more space. I gave up the idea of a bed of summer annuals, a fall border of dahlias and mums, a patch of naturalized spring bulbs. I knew that I would never be able to wave my hand and say, "Oh, that's my delphinium bed. There's not much going on there now, but you should see it in spring."

Instead, I decided to plant spring bulbs and fall bulbs and winter annuals and stolid succulents in all the borders. No part of the garden would be exclusively anything. That way, I would be able to make every spot look attractive in every season.

At least, that was the theory I came up with during that third winter. At the time, no part of my garden looked particularly attractive in *any* season. But I had set my goals and I was ready to try again, come spring.

Chapter Four
Sculpting a Garden

Using the Space

I spent the winter months scheming. By spring, I was eager to try out my new ideas. I wasn't exactly starting from scratch—dozens of plants already grew throughout the garden—but I might as well have been back at the beginning, because before the year was out I had moved nearly every plant in my garden.

First, I had to decide what to do with the space in the middle of the back yard. Only a few carrots, lettuce plants and mud-splattered pansies grew there, now. Since that first summer, when I dug sprawling vegetable beds in the center of my weed meadow, I'd decided that flowers should have the place of prominence in my garden. Still, I wasn't ready to give up the pleasure of harvesting my own fresh produce. After some thought, I decided to try growing vegetables in containers along the driveway on the south side of the house.

As it turned out, the edibles liked this out-of-the-way location. The sun reflecting off the cement was hotter than elsewhere in the yard. The dirt in the barrels was as rich as I could make it. And the drainage was perfect.

Moreover, I liked the vegetable garden's miniature size: it was just right for me. I found I could pack a lot of carrots into a wine barrel, so long as I didn't bother with rows. And I could grow plenty of snow peas if I trained them up a trellis.

With the vegetables out of the way, I could start planning what to do with all the empty space in the middle of the yard. My mother suggested filling the area with a big lawn, but I wanted to use the space in a more engaging way. I also hoped to use beds to disguise some of the yard's flaws.

The yard's odd shape was the main challenge. The gap left by the garage had changed the space from a rectangle-shape to a short, fat, upside down "L," with the house at the short end of the "L." (If you can picture the house as the period at the end of that sentence, you'll get the idea.)

An "L" was more interesting to work with than a plain box-shape, but it was also more complicated. The wide, fairly shallow configuration drew attention to the back fence. Standing on the deck outside the kitchen door, you couldn't help looking at that barrier of six-foot redwood boards. It looked like a movie screen or a chalk board. The fence seemed to be the focal point of the garden, rather than its boundary.

So I decided to create island beds in a diagonal line, coming from the far, right hand corner of the garden toward the narrower center. I hoped the trail of diagonal beds would draw attention away from the long back fence. I also hoped the plan would make the garden seem larger, since the diagonal line across the garden would be longer than its width or its length.

An Island Bed

First, I made a donut-shaped bed, not quite in the rear right hand corner of the garden, but almost. This bed covers most of the space where the garage once stood. I mounded up the soil slightly, then leveled the inside, giving the area a sense of enclosure. Sometime in the future, I meant to create a small patio there.

Into the ring of mounded soil, I cut two paths, the first coming in from the driveway, the second, at right angle to the first, leading out to the lawn (or where the lawn is now that I've planted it.) I set a bench flanked by pots of agapanthus across from the second path, facing the lemon tree across the yard.

I bought very few new plants that spring. Mostly, I moved around the plants I already had, leaving gaps for future purchases. I wanted to wait until I had a sense of the whole garden before I started filling the space with new flowers and shrubs. But I did buy a few trees.

For the donut bed, a star magnolia (*Magnolia stellata*) was my big extravagance. I planted it behind the bench, though it was still too short to cast shade. Then, after I had planted the tree, I could not resist putting a few more plants in the space immediately around it. I encircled the magnolia with a skirt of candytuft (*Iberis sempervirens* 'Purity'), partially to protect the magnolia's roots, which do not like to be disturbed, and partially because I knew that the snow-white candytuft would bloom in February at the same time as the magnolia. Then I went on to add a few white daffodils ('Mount Hood'), which also bloom in late winter.

During that makeover season, the donut bed was by far the nicest, least-raw part of my garden. The space inside the ring of mounded soil was peaceful and safe and reassuring. Paul and I liked to sit there, surrounded by the gently sloping earth.

While we were sitting there one day, Paul suggested I rename the donut bed. "Call it the womb chamber," he said. The term came from a book he was reading about religious architecture in India. He said it was a perfect name for a circular patio in the middle of a ring-shaped bed. After that, we always called the place our womb chamber.

The Pond

A few weeks later, I created another bed. This one lies more in the center of the garden, nudging up against the womb chamber. Together, they form one large vaguely figure-eight shaped bed. In the middle of this new bed, I dug a pond.

I meant for the pond to be quite big, with waterlilies blooming yellow and white, and a dramatic papyrus standing tall. I even imagined lotuses the size of tabletops floating on the surface of the water. But my clay soil made those plans impossible. My inexpensive shovel snapped like a toothpick in the thick dirt. My mother's fancier shovel lasted long enough for me to excavate a four-by-six-foot hole. But then my back went out. So I gave up.

What I ended up with is not the enormous pond I envisioned, but it is still a nice pond.

Framing a View

Next, I extended the diagonal line a little bit farther into the center of the garden with a jacaranda tree (*Jacaranda mimosifolia*). I chose a light, feathery tree that I knew would never block the view from the deck, but only filter it—tantalizingly, I hoped—through a tangle of ferny leaves and wisteria-blue flowers.

The Borders

My next task was to reshape the borders, since the ones I had drawn in flour were obviously too constricted. That spring, I widened all of the borders, especially the one on the north side of the yard. Sweeping around the lemon and quince trees, it is now substantial enough to balance the diagonal beds to the south. A slightly narrower border follows the back fence, and then the side fence, all the way to the driveway.

When I widened the borders, I also got rid of the sharp corners, creating smooth curves, instead. The additional space allows for groups of large shrubs to soften the right angles where the fence comes together. Finally, I added a new border by the deck. Together, these borders, with their softened corners, form another donut around the lawn.

Or seen another way, the island beds are a lumpy circle within the lumpy circle of the lawn within the lumpy circle of the borders, within the angles of my redwood fence.

Donuts or lumpy circles: either way it sounds unappetizing. But it looks fine. The design I came up with is simple without being boring.

Another strategy would have been to crowd the whole yard with plants, leaving just enough space for meandering paths and tiny garden rooms. I contemplated this plan, but I decided that the yard is too large for crowding—I could never have afforded all those plants!—and too small to hold a series of garden rooms. Though I decided not to create separate gardens, I did make a point of creating several different sections. The womb chamber, the pond, the area around the hammock, and the area around the deck are not physically blocked off from each other, but they form distinct spaces.

A Simple Path

After I had relocated some seventy-odd plants, and spread mulch over the new borders, I made a path going from the lawn (the future lawn) to the hammock hanging between the quince and lemon trees. I had some idea of how I wished the path to look. I wanted it to seem casual, even accidental. After all, a hammock is a casual feature, not like a stone bench or a fountain. So I settled on brick stepping stones.

They were easy to make. For each stepping stone, I dug a hole and lined it with sand, so that I could lay the bricks flush with the ground. I set eight bricks together, in two rows of four each, which is just the right size for a stepping stone.

Three of these stepping stones, surrounded by ajuga, lead to the hammock. They've been there for eight years now, without settling or shifting and are pleasingly unobtrusive stepping stones. Until you're standing on them, you hardly notice that they are there. But they're right where your feet want them to be.

A Cheap Patio

Now I was ready to start thinking about the patio I wanted to build in the center of the womb chamber. A friend gave me a hardscaping manual that he promised would tell me how to build paths and patios, walls and raised beds—in other words, the bones of the garden, the "hard" stuff. (Plants, I guess, are "soft.") This particular manual was full of very serious, architectural plans drawn in black and white alongside dazzling color photographs of the finished products.

"Just to give you some ideas," my friend said.

It gave me plenty of ideas, but none that I could carry out.

"High-quality hardscape is vital," the book declared.

It is also expensive. I didn't have much money to spend on the project, so when I'd finished mooning over the pictures of flagstone, old brick, and Mexican tiles, I put aside the book and bought a load of ordinary pink cement pavers.

The pavers aren't as awful as they sound. I improved them by breaking some of them in half. I remember my neighbor, Alan, goggling at me over the top of his hedge while I lifted the pavers out of the back seat of my convertible (a boatlike 1972 Cadillac de Ville) and smashed them on the sidewalk. He must have been dying to ask me what I was doing, but he restrained himself.

Actually, I wasn't surprised that Alan didn't speak. By then I had noticed that people in my neighborhood tended to keep to themselves. I could tell, though, that he was mystified to see me stoop down to check whether the pavers had broken into interesting shapes.

Once I had lugged the cement pavers into the back yard —whole or in pieces—I set them in sand, about half an inch apart, alternating broken pavers with whole ones. Used tidily, the pavers might have looked second-rate; but with rough, broken edges they became handsome in a rugged, urban sort of way. I suppose I could call the style "faux-recycled."

Once the pavers were all in place, I swept dirt into the cracks and planted the entire patio with creeping thyme

(*Thymus serpyllum coccineum*). Over the years, the pink cement has faded to a dull buff and the thyme has crept over the edges. I snip back the thyme twice during the summer, and that's all I do. I keep waiting for the groundcover to die out or go bald, as the books insist it must after a few years, but so far mine has not. It even has tolerated standing water and weeks of drought.

Hardscape That Says Too Much.

Sometimes I ask myself if stone would look better. I look at my path and my patio and wonder if the cheap materials make my garden look shoddy. I go back to the bookshelf and pull down that hardscaping manual again and compare my back yard to gardens furnished with gravel paths, brick walls, and raised beds made of railroad ties or even of corrugated metal.

I tell myself that those expensive materials add a lot of texture to a garden. In the end, though, I decide that they often add too much. The gardens end up being about stone and metal and wood, instead of dirt and leaves and flowers.

The big old estate gardens are different. They are works of art. They are fantasies. They are part of our shared culture. Elegant hardscape suits those gardens. The brick walls cloaked in ivy belong there as much as the tall, ancient trees do.

But sometimes in newly designed gardens, I think the hardscape overwhelms the plants. The gardens are no longer pleasant green and fragrant places for people to spend time, to linger and dream and talk, to escape themselves and also find themselves, to be absolutely *at home*. Instead, I think these spiffy gardens are meant to impress and even to intimidate a little. They say, "Aren't I something?" Whereas, successful gardens say nothing at all. They simply enfold you and make you feel safe.

Let me give an example on a very modest scale. In my mother's neighborhood, front walks made of crazy paving are very popular. For these front walks, the landscape architect takes out the straight cement walkway and sets down tray-sized flagstones in a sort of meandering path, and then surrounds the stones with pea-sized gravel or groundcover.

On a stroll around my mother's neighborhood recently, my mother and I passed just such a front garden. The stones were golden colored, large, gorgeous, and utterly "boughten looking." They simply did not blend with the environment at all.

My mother looked at the expensive walkway, and said "What a nice garden." I knew she wasn't talking about the tufts of native grasses plunked down in a perfunctory way on one side of the path. And she couldn't have been talking about the clump of lavender, as isolated and dead-looking as a rock, on the other side. She was talking about the stone. She was talking about money.

Maybe I'm just bellyaching because I can't afford such splendid stones myself, but I don't think so. When I enter my garden, I want the entire place to swallow me up and wrap me in tranquility. The garden needs to be a whole thing. Its individual features shouldn't jump out at me.

My patio floor satisfies me because it's innocuous. I hardly notice it, except when the thyme blooms, thick and purple, in June. And that's fine. I want people to walk on the patio, not stand and admire it. I want them to stroll across it and sit on the bench with me and look out at the pond and chat.

I think I understand what the designers want to achieve when they draw a garden in stone. They want a cohesive landscape. They know that plunging specimens into the ground is not the same as creating a garden. They know that growing a lot of healthy plants side by side is not enough. What they want to do is to design a garden. But often the designers depend on walkways and patios and walls to draw the garden together, instead of doing that job with plants.

I really can't blame them. They realize that when they leave the site, the owner of the garden may possibly kill all the plants. The walkways, though, will remain, so they concentrate on them.

In fact, the designers have every reason to worry about what the gardens will look like after they leave them, because usually the owners of these kinds of "done" gardens know nothing about plants. After a few months of neglect, even a maintenance-free landscape looks bad. The licorice plant has grown into a five-foot monster, the coreopsis needs deadheading, and the few annuals dotted around have died. Which only goes to show that all the hardscaping in the world cannot make an unloved garden look beautiful.

The Pond, Take Two

After I had finished the patio and decided I liked it, I looked at the rest of the island bed and found that something about the pond was wrong. I had encircled it with rocks, following the instructions in my water-garden encyclopedia, but I now I decided that the ring of stones looked heavy and unnatural—like a Camp Fire Girls fire pit. So I removed some of the rocks and set some of the others back in a staggered line. The arrangement became more or less, "Rock, rock, no rock, rock, set-back rock, rock, rock, no rock," and so on.

In the bare spaces, I planted clusters of hen-and-chicks (*Echeveria imbricata*) and patches of *Sedum acre*, even though one of my gardening books described the sedum as hopelessly invasive. In fact, I wanted an aggressive plant.

The sedum is perfect for the spot. The low, shaggy clumps dangle down into the pond, hiding the black plastic liner as effectively as the rocks once did. And the ropey arms embrace the large cabbagelike hen-and-chicks, creating a wonderful juxtaposition of textures and shades of grey. The sedum's roots are so shallow that I can tug out handfuls of the plant effortlessly when it creeps out of bounds.

The only problem I have with this evergreen (or evergray) plant is in July, when it rears up like a cobra and sprouts ugly yellow flowers on its tips. Why do so many gray plants bloom with muddy-yellow flowers? Dusty miller is another I can think of. I try to remember to cut off the sedum's flowering tips before they bloom.

When I rearranged the rocks around the pond, I put the largest ones closest to the womb chamber, arranging them to suggest a waterless waterfall. To add to the illusion, I planted tall flowers around the womb chamber. As a result, the back of the garden seems to slope up away above the front.

If I'd had the money, I suppose I might actually have changed the grade of the garden. But since the whole neighborhood is absolutely flat, a mountain in my backyard might look peculiar. I've seen mounds ("berms," I think they're called) plunked down indiscriminately in flat yards and they always look out of place. Instead, I created an illusion with plants and rocks.

From a distance, the round, thyme-covered patio in the center of the womb chamber, glimpsed through tall iris and roses and yarrow, looks a bit like a second pond beyond the first. It might even seem to be the pond's source of water.

I'm not trying to trick anyone, though. I don't want people to strain their imaginations over the pile of rocks and "see" a waterfall. Nor do I want people to look at my patio and think, "Ah, very pondlike." What I want is for people to feel, subconsciously, that my pond belongs there. I want them to sense that all the elements of my garden connect. What I don't want them to think is that my pond is nothing more than a hole in the middle of the garden.

Once I had finished fiddling with the pond's design, I was ready to plant it.

For water-plant containers, I reused one-gallon and five-gallon black plastic pots from the nurseries. I noticed that the catalogs sold special pots, but I decided they weren't necessary. I filled my recycled pots with my heaviest garden soil, from the north side of the house, and covered the soil with pebbles. That way, I was sure the plants would stay in place when I lowered the containers into the water.

To maneuver the pots into the pond, I had to climb down into the water first and then drag them in after me. It was wet, tiring work. Once the containers were in the water, though, they seemed lighter, and I could move them around until I found an arrangement I liked. First, I set a big clump of water iris (*Iris laevigata*) in the corner of the pond closest to the womb chamber. The iris serves several purposes: it ties the pond to the bed beyond and it emphasizes the diagonal axis of the garden. Its tall sabre leaves accentuate the verticality of the "dry waterfall" stones behind them.

After the iris, I added the water lilies. Though my tiny pond can only hold two, those two are magical. Magical, that is, when I manage to glimpse them open. Water lilies, unfortunately, bloom only during the day, a frustrating habit for gardeners who work from nine to five. And for some reason, the blossoms always seem to fade by the weekend.

I didn't want to buy a pump for my pond, so I put in lots of oxygenating plants, such as parrot's feather, which don't need pots at all. To 'plant' them, I just wrapped a lead ribbon around them, for a weight, and tossed the bunch into the water. As oxygenators, they work very well.

Within a week or two, all the living parts of the pond clicked into a functioning whole. The tiny sixty-nine cent goldfish from Woolworth's grew fat eating algae, and dragonflies darted out of nowhere to dine upon the mosquito larvae that thrashed frantically on the surface of the water. Big orange dragonflies hovered above the water, mirroring the goldfish swimming below. Smaller blue ones perched on the tips of the green iris leaves, imitating flowers.

Those dragonflies especially pleased me. I never had seen them in my garden before. How had they known to come? "My pond must really be a pond," I thought, "and not just a hole in ground, if the dragonflies take it seriously."

A Brazen Fantasy

Today, the garden looks much less boxy than it did when I first began working on it nearly a decade ago. And yet, there's a limit to what I can do with the space. It remains a small fenced-in yard, and it always will. My neighbor's clothesline will always stretch above my back fence, squeaking loudly when the neighbor pulls in his dry laundry—usually at ten or eleven at night. And my other neighbor's garage will always loom on the north side of the garden, behind the quince and lemon trees.

In a sense, my garden is a container garden. Working on it is like tending a garden in a huge pot. The container is the fence of course, and in a larger sense, it's also the neighborhood and even the entire city.

I never try to pretend that my garden is anything more than a garden in a box. Although I soften the corners of the fence with shrubs, I let my flowers grow smack up against the cracked concrete driveway, without trying to hide the concrete or soften the transition.

In a way, I'm glad my yard is such an artificial space. It gives me an opportunity to create an unabashed fantasy within its boundaries. I feel no scruples about using non-native plants in my garden. I mingle South African corms with Mediterranean herbs, creating a combination that has never existed in the natural world. And I do it without guilt, knowing that after all a back yard never existed in the natural world either.

When I come across horticulture books urging me to, "Create a garden that suits the landscape and plays up the natural features of the land," I respond, "But I can't create a landscape that suits the natural features of the garden, because there are no natural features in my garden!"

And yet, in a way, the fence and the driveway themselves are natural features, just as a hillside or a creek or a patch of desert or old growth trees might be features of a rural garden. The fence and the driveway are what I have been given. They're what I have to work with.

I wonder why more garden writers haven't yet caught on to the fact that many, many gardeners all over the country garden in small, boxy back yards. I suspect that far more of us exist than gardeners with mountains and creeks near our back doors. And though some of us might live in the suburbs, we don't all want to create suburban back yards with concrete pads and swimming pools and barbecue grills. We want something more magical than that.

We don't quite want urban gardens, either, although they can be wonderful. I've visited marvelous, tiny gardens behind Victorian row houses in San Francisco. The best are usually formal affairs, with brick patios, rosemary or ivy topiaries in urns, elegant fountains, and lots of foliage plants. Often they are paved, with plants in containers. And usually they are geometric in design, with symmetrically placed pots and angular lines. I imagine that small urban gardens in New York or New Orleans or Seattle are similar, in essence, to the ones I have seen in San Francisco, even if the plants and the materials of the hardscape vary in the different regions.

Such a formal style isn't quite what we back yard gardeners want, either. The style is too expensive to be practical in any but the tiniest gardens. Although, its jewel-like perfection suits those small spaces, it's essentially an urban style.

What do gardeners with average-sized fenced yards want? Perhaps some of them want what I want: a garden that's too stylized to be called natural and too unruly to be called formal. For example, I want a few big things in my small yard: at least one big tree and some big flowers. Most of all, though, I want a certain largeness of spirit. I want extravagance. Romance. Adventure.

And I want a lawn.

The Lawn

In the matter of lawns, I feel like the king in the A.A. Milne poem who wants some butter for his breakfast bread. The dairy maid and the queen and even the cow try to persuade the king that marmalade is very popular and just as good as butter. But the king repeats plaintively, "I do like a little bit of butter to my bread." In the same way, I do like a little bit of lawn for my garden. Raked gravel, though very nice in some places, just isn't the same.

From the very beginning, I planned on having a lawn in my garden. After I finished designing the new borders, I was finally ready to put it in. But just when I was about to order the sod from the nursery, the local newspaper ran an article about the evils of grass.

The journalist who wrote the article was clever. He knew that the best way to influence gardeners is to ridicule them, so he wrote about how conventional lawns have become, how suburban, how cliched. He counted on the fact that no one wants to be conventional.

In place of grass, the journalist recommended low-maintenance, drought-resistant groundcovers. After I read the article, I walked around town looking for examples of these lawn-free gardens. Once I began looking for them, I saw them everywhere. In fact, I found so many that I felt able to make one myself, should I decide to do without a lawn after all.

First, I would have to buy a lot of plants. I would have to be sure, however, not to buy *too* many, for this type of garden must always look slightly spartan.

Next, I would have to dot these plants around the yard, about three or four feet apart, with no relation to each other.

Then I would need to lay down lots of ugly black tubing. The drip irrigation system is always ostentatiously ugly in this kind of landscape. Once the tubing was in place, I would need to cover everything with expensive mulch. (Of course, if I had purchased more plants, I would not have to spend so much money on mulch, but never mind.) Unfortunately, the mulch in these gardens never quite hides the black tubing. But that's okay, too. The bits of plastic peeking out will show everyone how virtuous I am and how much money I have spent on my new irrigation system.

This is what I *could* have done, if I'd decided to follow the journalist's advice. Needless to say, I didn't. I was stubborn when I designed my garden. I planted a lawn, and let other people blemish their yards with groundcover gardens. As far as I could see, too many of those eyesores existed already.

Today, even more of them exist. The groundcover garden is becoming as conventional in California as the front yard lawn.

The worst aspect of the groundcover hodgepodges is that they don't act as a foil to other beds. The mats of *Vinca minor* and snow-in-summer and gazanias and various thymes and sedums grow together into what people flatteringly call a "tapestry." In reality, the plants form a flat blanket that manages to be dull and chaotic at the same time.

This jumble of groundcovers becomes the main feature of the garden. If a gardener tries to use the groundcovers as a conventional lawn, backing them up either with a border of drought-resistant shrubs or with traditional foundation plantings, the result looks even more muddled.

Conventional or not, nothing else complements beds and borders quite as perfectly as a lawn. I'm glad I included one when I designed my garden. Today, when I stroll through my back yard, I see the borders—not the area between the borders. My restful green lawn flatters the other plants around it, without ever calling attention to itself, the way a patch of ice plant would.

I don't believe my lawn sucks up more than its share of the world's resources. For one thing, I never fertilize it. I don't need to give my lawn anything, because I never take anything away from it. Instead of harvesting a crop of grass tips every week, I let the clippings remain on the surface, to rot back in again. I let Benedict the guinea pig and Henry the rabbit graze on the lawn and add their bits of fertilizer. I water deeply every three weeks or so in the summer. That's all I do.

Although I sound very pro-grass, Paul used to suspect me of fostering a plot against our lawn, because every autumn I killed sections of it. When I reconfigured the borders that third spring, I made them too narrow (again!). Luckily, they were easy to widen. Not bothering to dig out the grass, I simply covered it with newspapers and piles of leaves from my neighbor's liquidambar tree. Then I weighed everything down with some of my own half-rotted compost.

The effect was not much uglier than bare dirt would have been.

After I spread the compost, I left the area alone. Worms and pill bugs and four months of rain did the rest of the work. By the time the ground had dried out enough to work, the grass had turned to soil.

When I planted the new section of the border, I didn't even turn over the earth; I just dug holes for the plants. Only the green plastic net that tangled around my trowel as I dug reminded me that sod had lain there once.

Killing the grass was the easy part. Rearranging the plants was more of a hassle. Basically, I moved everything forward. In one spot, for instance, the candytuft went where the grass had been, the penstemon moved in where the candytuft had grown, and so on, until a space by the fence opened up for the nice tall shrubby plant I should have put in to begin with.

The result of all this border thickening was, of course, lawn shrinkage. Sod originally covered half the yard. Today, grass grows on less than a third of the ground. It is still, I think, big enough for a child to have plenty of fun. I'm sure Leo will spend as much time on it as I do. The lawn I have now is roomy enough for a picnic, for stretching on out with a book, or for tossing around a ball, but not wide enough to seem static, like an empty room. Around the womb chamber, it's little more than a path. But that threading loop of green unites the garden and brings peace to it.

I don't expect to remove any more lawn; I like it as it is. And I know that I never will replace it with a carpet of pumpkin-colored gazanias and purple-flowered ice plant.

Meanwhile, in the Front Yard

We certainly didn't need to plant a lawn in the front yard. When we bought our house, tough, shaggy Bermuda grass covered most of the ground from the sidewalk to the house. Paul and I dug out some of the Bermuda grass on each side of the front walk, both along the foundation and near the sidewalk. In the middle, we left enough Bermuda grass for a rugged, if rather invasive, front lawn. Every few months, I pull its creeping arms away from the fuchsias and the other plants in the borders.

Those four new borders started out straight and edged in brick. I agonized over that brick edging and finally removed it, deciding that I preferred the look of an edged lawn or, in some places, the extravagance of plants spilling out of the borders onto the grass.

The Pergola

One day in winter, I stood at the back door watching the rain fall on the lawn. In three years my backyard had changed remarkably, but some things remained the same. For one thing, I hadn't managed to get rid of all the weeds. Onion grass and sour grass still popped up here and there in the sunny parts of the borders. And I knew that in the dusky spaces between the daylilies and the agapanthus, sly, fierce blackberry vines still twined along the ground.

Compared to the vigorous weeds, some of the newly planted—or newly transplanted—perennials looked vulnerable and insignificant. The garden still seemed a bit flat and empty. It needed a focus, something with an imposing presence, something tall. The lemon and quince trees provided height on the north side, but the south side depended on a lilliputian star magnolia. And it just wasn't doing its job.

Right then, I decided that Paul and I had to do something. "We need to build a pergola. *Now.*"

Winter is a good time to build in California. The weather is too cold for eating outdoors or for reading in the sun, but not too cold for dragging around lumber and wielding hammers. So that month—in between rain storms—Paul and I built a pergola over the womb chamber.

Paul designed the pergola to be quite tall, more than ten feet high. I was skeptical at first. But he told me that over-building would be better than under-building, and I think he was right.

Next to the pergola, I planted a climbing hydrangea (*Hydrangea petiolaris*). Like the star magnolia, it's a slow grower. It still has a long way to climb, but in the meantime, the bare pergola makes a substantial statement on its own. On sunny days, the lattice throws a fretwork of shadows over the grass, and the structure itself is so lovely, in a way, that I will almost be sorry when dark, heavy leaves obscure it.

Pots

During the winter, I also created a container garden on the deck. I had noticed that the kitchen window looked out mostly on bare wood. And since the weather was forcing us to spend more time indoors, I thought the view might as well be pretty.

For easy maintenance, I bought big, plain clay pots and filled them with big, plain plants—one variety per pot. I had no time for neurotic arrangements of lobelia, ivy geranium, and artemisia, with something tufty in the middle.

Instead of buying a lot of new plants, I used divisions of plants I already had. Architectural foliage plants, including fountains of agapanthus, strappy naked ladies (*Amaryllis belladonna*), jagged, tiered acanthuses, and swordlike ferns, went into the largest pots around the edges of the deck. More delicate plants, either succulents or groundcovers, went into smaller pots in front of the large ones.

Many of the plants, such as lavender, curry plant (*Helichrysum angustifolium*), and lemon thyme (*Thymus citriodorus*), offered fragrance, as well as attractive foliage. Others, including African daisies and calla lilies, flowered ceaselessly throughout the season.

The plants I chose for my container garden are common plants, but they do not seem ordinary, because they are in smaller portions. A six-inch circle of *Sedum acre* in a pot looks more distinguished than a three-foot-long drift in the garden. It mounds up nicely in a container, looking like a grayish wig. Even simple, unpretentious groundcovers such as candytuft or gazania seem extravagant trailing over the edges of a pot.

Groundcovers and succulents make ideal pot plants because they divide so easily. I literally ripped hunks of ajuga, snow-in-summer, and different sedums from inconspicuous spots in my borders and plunged them right into my pots.

Of all the potted groundcovers, I am especially fond of the ajuga, because it reminds me of when I first met the plant long ago, in the slick pages of a plant encyclopedia. Back then, I could not distinguish between the diminutive blue-flowered groundcover and the majestic azure-spiked delphinium. Since that time I have become very friendly with ajuga. (I've never grown as familiar with delphinium, unfortunately.) Green-leaved ajuga edges some of my borders. Bronze-leaved ajuga runs through the peach border, weaving the other plants together. *Ajuga* 'Burgundy Glow' creeps under cape mallow, echoing the shrub's pink flowers. I know ajuga well. Ajuga is vigorous. Ajuga is common. I definitely take ajuga for granted.

And yet, it isn't bad looking. My white porcelain pot calls attention to the plant's small paddle-shaped leaves, sleek as a reptile's scales. The pot is like a frame, making a lovely picture out of a common groundcover. And when those diminutive blue minarets rise in early spring, I remember why I once mistook ajuga for a nobler plant.

A Rose Border

Late one afternoon in December, as I sat on the deck absorbing the last thin rays of sun, I found myself wishing for a visual boundary between myself and the rest of the yard, something to partly enclose the deck. Since winter is prime rose-planting time, I thought of roses.

A few days later, I planted a line of bare root 'Iceberg' floribunda roses in the border along the deck. I knew that when they grew up, the shrubs would edge the deck with a hedge of white flowers, while the bases would block out the dark cobwebby space underneath it.

The border is in such a prominent place, I decided that it ought to look good in every season. To make sure it did, I mixed in some bulbs and corms, including cyclamin, naked ladies, ixia, and spraxsis, planted under a blanket of snow-in-summer.

The Greenhouse

The greenhouse was the last major feature we added to the garden. Its erection marked the end of the construction phase in the garden's life and the beginning of the long, slow development phase—a phase that has not ended yet.

Paul and I had been searching for a way to hide some of our unused driveway, which runs along the side of the house, and thrusts oddly into the garden, leading to a garage that is no longer there. Containers of vegetables cover much of the driveway near the sidewalk. We needed a way to incorporate the other end of the driveway into the back yard's overall design.

Paul was the one who thought of using the slab of unsightly concrete as a greenhouse floor. Besides giving me a place to start seeds and stash my trowel, it would shelter us from the street, which was a good thing. Paul was getting tired of people on the sidewalk peering down the driveway at us when we sat in the womb chamber, reading or eating our dinner. The greenhouse walls would blur us to the passersby.

Our greenhouse came by mail order, in fragments. The first time we picked up our glass at the warehouse, we found our boxes under someone else's crates of computer monitors. At least a third of the panes were broken, so we ordered more. About a third of those arrived broken. And so on. We kept ordering more glass and the greenhouse company kept sending it.

Since two months passed before we got our hands on enough unbroken panes to complete the greenhouse, we just put up the aluminum frame and added the glass as it arrived. When, eventually, we completed the job, we both agreed that the greenhouse was a wonderful thing to have: a privacy screen for Paul; an official puttering place for me.

I loved setting up my stuff on the potting table we built. I arranged the bag of potting soil next to the box of seeds, stacked my pots according to size, and set the bottles of insecticidal soap and fish emulsion and sunspray oil all in a row on the floor. The trowel and the clippers lay in a wooden box. The shovel leaned against the wall. It was like my playhouse laboratory all over again, only I didn't torture earthworms any more.

After I set up the greenhouse, I ran around the garden taking cuttings of candytuft and lantana and abutilon and star jasmine and everything else I could think of. Not that I needed twenty 'Confetti' lantana or had space for a dozen more 'Apricot Glow' abutilons, but I liked to arrange the cuttings in boxes of sand, next to the jars of water holding cuttings from my fuchsias and spider plants.

That winter, when my greenhouse was new, I read a very fancy gardening book by a woman with a large estate in England. She declared that every truly great garden must contain a body of water and an outbuilding. Her declaration made me smile, because I knew that my garden fit the bill—assuming I could call a four-by-six foot pond a "body of water," and an eight-by-ten-foot greenhouse an "outbuilding." And I did call them that. I didn't care if they were small, for I knew they were in scale with my small garden.

Finished?

Hardly.

But after we built the greenhouse, I stopped adding new elements to the garden. "Know when to stop," I told myself. And for once, I listened.

The garden I had created was just one of many that would have worked in my backyard. Often I fantasized about other gardens. I envisioned a witty, formal, terribly contrived Tudor garden. I saw a sunny meadow, a lush tropical extravaganza, a grove of majestic sequoias. And yet, I decided that the garden I had was fine for now. It pretty well answered the question, "What can you do with a small, flat, boxy backyard if you don't have a lot of money to spend?"

The design was complete only in the most general sense. A framework had emerged from the blur, and was slowly shaping into something I could call a garden. The outline was fixed, but the interiors of the borders and beds had only begun to evolve.

As a gardener, I still had a lot to learn. But those three years of hands-on work had taken me far from the libraries and bookstores where I had started my education.

I was beginning to be familiar with the act of gardening —the whole yearlong cycle. The familiarity was something in my body, as well as in my mind. My shoulders were used to shoveling, now. And my arms knew how to saw. My fingers knew how to perform the delicious task of "muddying in" a new transplant. In twelve or so months, I had changed as much as my back yard had.

When Paul found me in the kitchen, muttering curses about a rose thorn in my thumb or wrapping band-aids around my forefinger where the teeth of a pruning saw had sunk deep into the flesh, he assumed that all the "changes" I talked about were nothing more than a collection of wounds. When I asked him to rub my shoulders at night, after a day of spreading compost, he was sure that gardening was about discovering new forms of self-abuse. But he was wrong.

It was about pride; about learning to do something well. I was proud of my scars and my sore muscles. I was proud of my garden. Most of all I was proud of myself for becoming a real foul-mouthed, callous-fingered, somewhat knowledgeable, sometimes dreamy, but generally hard-working gardener.

Chapter Five
Two Lessons

Stumbling Onward—The Fourth Year

By the fourth year, the design had jelled. The outlines
of the garden beds and borders satisfied me, forming nice
shapes, nice blocks of space. When I stood on the deck and
squinted out at the garden through half-closed eyes, I felt
quite proud.

When I opened my eyes, however, my heart sank. Within
those pleasing outlines, the plantings still looked spotty and
chaotic. The best thing, in fact, that could be said about the
jumble of perennials and annuals and shrubs was that they
were alive.

Three years before, that would have been enough. A
garden full of vigorous plants was all I asked for—in the beginning. But by the fourth year, growing healthy plants was
less of a challenge for me. I took those vigorous plants for
granted. I wanted something more than that.

By this time, I had stopped reading how-to books and
plant encyclopedias, and had started poring over books
about other people's gardens. My head was full of pictures
of Christopher Lloyd's Great Dixter, of Sissinghurst, or—
closer to home—California's own Filoli. Those wondrous
gardens taught me that the interiors of my borders could be

more than an unrelated collection of bright, flourishing flowers. The plants could—and should—fit together in a pleasing whole.

Focal Points in the Borders

That fourth year I worked hard to bring order, harmony, and beauty to my jumble of rugged plants. Often I felt frustrated. My standards were rising quickly and I doubted whether my gardening skills would ever catch up. Luckily, I made two important discoveries that year. One was about structure and the other was about color.

The first discovery—a revelation, really—came to me early one morning in March, as I was picking the newspaper out of a patch of shrubs and ferns on the north side of the front yard. I was proud of that green, shady corner of the garden. It seemed complete in a way that other areas did not. And as I stood there in my pajamas, I took a minute to figure out why.

"It's the pyracanthas!" I said to myself.

It was suddenly clear to me that the row of pyracanthas gave the border its appealing structure. "How clever of me to have put them in," I thought.

Then I remembered that the attractive planting scheme had come about accidently, like many of the garden's successes. The pyracanthas were among the few plants that had come with the house. They were only there now because I hadn't known how to kill them.

The first time Paul and I explored our new property, I looked at those shrubs and said, "The thorny things are awful." Of course, they looked much different back then. Each one was about five feet tall, dense and tangled, with cobwebs growing creepily over evil-looking barbs. My mother told me that under the right circumstances, pyracanthas could make attractive espaliers, but I decided that mine were too overgrown to become much of anything. So after Paul and I moved in, I sawed off the trunks a few inches above the ground.

In those early months, fixing up the inside of the house preoccupied me. I didn't often think of the garden. And so when I finally turned my attention to the front yard, I was surprised to see hundreds of suckers growing out of the sawed ends. Since I knew very little about the root systems of shrubs, I had assumed they would simply "go away." But they had not gone away. The shrubs were quite alive. I couldn't afford to pay someone to grind up the stumps, so I decided to make use of them. With my brand-new garden clippers, I snipped those suckers into plump green spheres.

My mother cringed the first time she saw my new topiaries. "They look like basketballs," she said.

And she was right. But those fat green basketballs helped me organize the rest of the border. Months later, when I planted the front yard, I said to myself, "Hmm, I'll tuck an abutilon behind that pyracantha and some ferns on the side. Now what should go in front?" And I was off.

That March morning of the fourth spring, I suddenly understood that the problem with my other borders was I had not shaped them around key plants. I had tried four of this and a row of that and a clump of something else. In some spots, I had muddled my way toward a satisfactory design. In other places, I never had managed a coherent plan. In *every* place, the process had been more difficult and frustrating than it ought to have been.

Now, suddenly, those pyracanthas gave me the inspiration I was looking for. That morning, as I stood in the front yard in my pajamas, soggy newspaper in hand, I decide to set core plants in all the borders before the season was over. They would have to be constant plants; evergreen and slow growing like the pyracanthas.

Once they were in place, I'd be able to work outward from those focal points, shaping the borders around them. The focal points would lend structure to fairly informal planting schemes, but more importantly they would help me structure my thinking. In other words, the focal points would organize my brain as much as organize the borders.

The North Border: Semi-symmetry

In the back yard, I rearranged the north border first, because it already contained its focal point. The lemon and quince trees, with the hammock between them, formed a sort of tableau in the center of the border. The rest of the border would stretch out from this midpoint.

First I placed a pair of boxwood plants (*Buxus*), a few feet away from the trees, and clipped their shaggy foliage into spheres. These dark dense little balls of boxwood have turned out to be surprisingly powerful accents. As you gaze down the border, they stop your glance and hold it still for a moment.

Then your eyes move on to the focal points I planted next: two spiky clumps of spider plants, which lie a bit farther out from the trees. The jagged shapes of these plants look like little explosions in the middle of the border. They move the eye, pushing it outward toward other plants.

The two sets of focal points are very different, yet they both manage to organize the border. The other more unassuming plants around them gain character from these pairs of foliage plants.

I did not, however, want the whole border to be rigidly symmetrical. Except in a few key places, I tried to get away with symmetry that is barely symmetrical. For instance, at the front of the border, lamb's ears (*Stachys lanata*) and snow-in-summer (*Cerastium tomentosum*) balance each other effectively. Although they are not identical plants, their similar gray color suggests an echo.

When I planted the border, I also depended on plants with similar shapes to mirror each other. This is cheating, of course. But when the fraud is successful the harmony is subtle—a blur in the corner of the eye, something felt more than seen.

For example, in the mid border, I put in a clump of society garlic (*Tulbaghia violacea*) to repeat the shape of a miniature white agapanthus (*Agapanthus africanus* 'Henryi'). Both plants throw out fountains of narrow arching leaves and hold their flowers high above the foliage. The garlic looks more delicate, but the two plants are enough alike to mirror each other well.

In a few places, I set two plants together and then created a similar relationship between two other plants elsewhere in the border. For example, on one side, I let a hardy geranium (*Geranium* 'Wargave Pink') with flowers of palest pink roam around beneath a white *Salvia greggii*. On the other side, I tucked creeping 'Confetti' lantana with flowers that range from pink and orange to peach, beneath a 'coral' *Salvia greggii*.

The South Border—Edible Landscaping

After I had rearranged the border on the north side of the garden, I started on the one across the yard. Here, unfortunately, there were no convenient pyracantha or fruit trees to get me going. I had to organize the border myself, from scratch.

Instead of splitting the border into halves radiating out from a central focus, I decided to divide the border into fourths and plant big, gray-green artichoke plants to mark those sections. I already had three of them crowded among the other vegetables in the driveway, languishing in their pots. The big plants proved to be fine focal points in the border. They're large architectural plants, as striking as yuccas or giant agaves. Everything else nearby looks better because of them. And best of all, they produce artichokes—more than ten per plant during a season.

In *The Complete Book of Edible Landscaping*, Rosalind Creasy suggests leaving some of the artichokes on the plant to bloom. I'm usually too greedy to do that. I want to eat my artichokes. But that first spring I left a couple on the plant to mature. The spectacle of those huge purple thistles inspired me to build the entire border around purple-flowered, grey-leaved plants. Since the border is sunny and exposed, I also tried to chose unthirsty plants whenever I could.

The flowers I added include bearded iris, more society garlic, betony (*Stachys officinalis*)—a relative of lamb's ears, but with prettier flowers—shrubby, perennial wallflower (*Erysimum* 'Bowles Mauve'), and a favorite of mine, *Sedum spectabile*, 'Brilliant.'

Similar to its more popular cousin, *Sedum* 'Autumn Joy,' this sedum blends well with other plants all season long. Its platelike flowerheads start out ice green in July. In August, they turn a pale sugary pink, intensifying slowly to rose-purple as the month progresses. In September, they fade to buff and linger until Halloween.

I also included a few purple flowers with green leaves, including *Liatris spicata* 'Kobold,' obedient plant (*Physostegia virginiana*), and common chives.

(There were other colors, too, when I first started out, and plants that just had to go—but more of that later. I'm concerned with the focal points now, and with the parts of the borders that have not changed in years.)

To complete the plantings, I added a few perennials from elsewhere in the garden. Calla lilies, and *Boltonia asteroides* 'Snowbank' bloom in back. Candytuft and lamb's ears spread out in front. These plants tie the area into the rest of the garden, and prevent it from looking like a set-piece dropped down against the fence.

For additional structure, against the fence, at intervals between the artichokes, I planted two plum trees and a nectarine tree. When the trees were young, they looked spindly and ridiculous, as though I had pinned them to the wall because they couldn't stand up on their own. Now, after more than half a decade, they've grown into real espaliers, with good strong lines.

Shortly after I planted the border, purple-flowered morning glory (*Ipomoea purpurea*) invited itself onto the fence. At first, I was distressed to see the vine there. I knew that I'd have a task controlling it. Morning glory, I'd discovered, is the kudzu of the west. Chopping it back only encourages it to grow faster. Even when a hard frost knocks it to the ground, (which happens every five years or so) it springs back quickly.

"There goes my border," I thought, when I saw the stems twisting over the top of the fence. Since then I've tried to learn to live in peace with the morning glory. Although I tear it out of the trees and yank it out of the beds, I don't pull it entirely off the fence. I let it billow over in heavy tangles of heart-shaped leaves, purple flowers, and cordlike stems.

That south border—with its shaggy, leafy fence and big artichoke plants, looks informal, no doubt about it. The casual stroller might not even notice the structure, but it's there. And I think it seeps into the visitor's mind—or soul, or whatever part of a person it is that responds to a garden.

The Back Border: Abundance and Restraint

For the long border along the back fence, I needed a large focal point. What I ended up with was not a focal point at all, but an area of contrasting styles. In this border, I decided to mix formal and informal features. I would crowd the sides of the border with large, unpretentious shrubs. Then, in the center of the border, I would train star jasmine (*Trachelospermum jasimoides*) into diamond patterns on the fence.

Since I wanted the shrubs to form a frame around the center of the border, the two sides needed to balance each other. The task was not simple. I needed shade-lovers to group against the north end of the fence near the lemon tree, and drought-tolerant specimens for the other end of the border, which is quite exposed and arid. I also needed to create similar compositions out of these dissimilar plants.

On the shady side, I introduced an oakleaf hydrangea (*Hydrangea quercifolia*), with leaves that turn a glorious reddish orange in autumn—even in Berkeley's mild climate. In front of the hydrangea, I placed several *Anemone japonica* 'Alba.'

The hydrangea and the Japanese anemones both have jagged heart-shaped foliage, so the composition looks interesting even when the plants are out of bloom. Into the midst of this abundant foliage, I slipped a single shade-tolerant rose bush 'Gruss an Aachen.' In April, and then again in

June, and October, the rose's peachy-white blossoms glow among green leaves, brightening this shady corner of the garden.

For the sunny side, I chose a pink-flowered oleander (*Nerium oleander*) instead of a hydrangea, and a few pink-flowered cape mallows (*Anisodontea capensis*). In front of the shrubs, I added a mounding, gray leaved licorice plant (*Helichrysum*).

I also wanted a couple of easygoing plants that would be happy on both sides of the border, in either sun or shade. Abutilons worked well for me in both spots. (In hotter climates than mine, though, abutilons might wilt in full sun.) For the south side, I chose a white-flowering abutilon. For the other side, I selected a variety called 'apricot glow.' These tall, airy plants—too treelike to be called shrubs, too shrublike to be trees—bracket the border gracefully.

Once the larger plants were in place, I found it easier to add some smaller ones. For leaf contrast, I studded the space between the oakleaf hydrangea and the Japanese anemones with quill-like ferns. Beneath the white abutilon I planted wine cups (*Callirhoe involucrata*). Under the peach abutilon, I planted pale orange nasturtiums. The nasturtiums and the wine cups creep over the ground and weave everything together.

In the center of the border, I planted two more licorice plants, and three smokebushes (*Continus coggygria purpurus*), pruned back hard to form short, dense, shrubs. Purple fountain grass (*Pennisetum setaceum* 'Rubrum') adds a vertical contrast to the mounding shrubs, a razor-narrow contrast to the round-leaved plants, and brings another spot of burgundy into the border. Dark green candytuft, gray lamb's ears, and mahogany flowered gazanias edge the planting.

Finally, I planted the jasmine against the fence. The vine's glossy dark green leaves contrast with the grey plants and echo the candytuft's deep green foliage. In cold weather, a scattering of jasmine leaves turns crimson, a nice counterpoint to the reddish grass below. Best of all, the diamond shapes insert an element of unabashed artificiality.

I suppose I could have done without the jasmine diamonds, and hidden the entire length of fence behind shrubby plants. But I think the shrubs alone would have looked perfunctory. The border would have been big, healthy, lush —and dumb. The diamonds give the border wit.

To me, formal elements show that a mind is at work in a garden as well as a back and a pair of arms. Of course gorgeous, blowzy "wild" gardens require brainwork, too. They can be as hard to create and as challenging to maintain as a formal landscape. But formal elements nevertheless signal more obviously that here an artist has dared to shape nature. Formal elements can be pompous or funny, somber or elegant.

The formal element certainly doesn't dominate the border, though. At its edges, for instance, the neat jasmine fades into a slightly out-of-control profusion of shrubiness. In fact, I think of the border's mix of the formal and informal as an illustration of the tension in a garden between artifice and nature. To me that tension is very appealing: it is, I think, the essence of gardening.

Transplanting

Or perhaps the real "essence of gardening" is sweat. It certainly was for me that spring. Refocusing my borders meant digging up a lot of plants and lugging them around the garden, work that was strenuous and dirty and very down to earth.

One result of all this work was that I became an expert at transplanting. I learned the importance of digging big.

First, you must dig a big hole to get as much of the root ball as possible. A plant doesn't do well if you leave half of its root system in a border across the garden. Then you must dig another big hole, large enough to receive the plant. There's no point trying to stuff a big root ball into a small hole.

Once or twice that spring I ignored my own advice and tried to build up the dirt around the top of a root ball that bulged up out of a hole that was too small. But I soon learned that cheating doesn't work. Gardening is a life and death activity, and a cheated plant usually dies.

I also learned the importance of watering very well—filling the hole with water before a plant goes in, and drenching the soil afterward.

Throughout the early part of spring, I transplanted feverishly. Then, during the spring's flowery climax, and through the long dry summer, I put away my shovel and my trowel and left the plants alone.

When the weather cooled in fall, I started digging and hauling and planting again. Only this time my obsession was not structure. This time I was preoccupied with color.

Color Scheming

On the subject of color I was a slow learner. I managed to limit the kinds of plants I grew—cutting out inappropriately thirsty or tender plants, for instance—long before I learned to limit the color of the plants I grew.

The problem was, I liked all the colors in my garden. Apricot roses, scarlet dahlias, yellow coreopsis, purple salvia —I liked them all. And I liked variegated foliage, silver leaved plants and wine-red grasses, too. Every leaf or blade or flower in my garden looked pretty to me. I hated to remove any of them.

That third autumn, however, I decided to revise my color scheme, not because I thought my garden was ugly, but because I felt that it could be more attractive. Once again, I learned from the famous gardens I encountered in those glossy books. The illustrations taught me to see color in an entirely new way.

I saw a dazzling display of apricot roses with orange cannas and bladelike, peach-striped New Zealand flax (*Phormium tenax*) in Christopher Lloyd's garden. I saw cool arrangements of green and white hostas and variegated phlox in Pamela J. Harper's garden. I saw pink tulips set beneath blooming fruit trees in the garden of Joe Eck and Wayne Winterrowd.

I knew of course that I could never recreate those exact combinations. Not all of the plants in those east coast or English gardens would suit the California climate. But I could learn from the spirit of those plantings.

More than anything else, my glimpses of those great gardens taught me that real beauty comes from combinations of plants, not from the beauty of individual blossoms. Those pictures convinced me that a pair of undistinguished flowers can look breathtaking together, if they've been sensitively coupled. (Conversely, two perfectly attractive flowers can turn ugly side by side, if they don't belong together.)

The key to successful combinations is color. Once I understood that, I was maddened by the fact that my garden was a whirling washing machine of tousled hues. I wasn't getting the best from my flowers. I was wasting their beauty.

I already had a color scheme, of sorts, but it was not successful. The border on the south side of the garden was the purple border; the womb chamber mostly contained yellow flowers; and I called the border on the north side the apricot border, although it included blues and whites as well. Obviously, I had too many colors in too many places.

So I started moving plants again. The first thing I did was to eliminate yellow from the back yard. One cool September afternoon, I dug up all my coreopsis, 'Moonshine' yarrow, and 'Stella d'Oro' daylilies. Soon chunks of dirt and roots and leaves covered the lawn. "Now what do I do with them?" I wondered. I couldn't bear to throw away healthy plants, so I set the yellow flowers in large containers in the driveway with the vegetables. "A temporary arrangement," I said.

They are still there today, a regular part of the scenery. That container garden has become a place for flowers in exile, as well as a place to grow vegetables. It's where flowers go when they've been ejected from the rest of the garden, either because their colors are hard to use well or because their growth is too rampant for the borders. In these pots, a blinding orange-red pelargonium blooms next to an aggressive, pink Four-O'-Clock (*Mirabilis jalapa*). A difficult, rust-orange gazania flowers in the same pot with a very assertive mint. And here, most of the yellow flowers that used to grow in the back yard bask in reflected light, dazzling away happily among other hot colored flowers, and pots of tomatoes and peppers and cucumbers.

After I moved the yellows, I reorganized the pinks. I realized, a bit belatedly, that all pinks are not alike. Once again, a border in the front yard taught me a lesson that I should have learned years ago. It was a pink border, near the sidewalk. A dozen different kinds of drought-resistant pink flowers bloomed together there, billowing over the property line. The border included *Gaura lindheimeri*, *Penstemon* 'Elfin Pink,' *Saliva Greggii* 'Raspberry,' *Geranium* 'Wargave Pink,' and others. Mostly, it looked fine. But one pink pelargonium stood out oddly.

One evening, in October of that third year, I plucked a blossom from the misfit plant and wandered around the garden with it, Vita Sackville-West style, trying to decide where the pelargonium belonged. To my surprise, I found that the blossom looked far better in the peach border than it had in the pink border.

Although I'd read about the difference between hot and cool colors, I hadn't really grasped what that difference meant. But when I saw the way that the pelargonium, which had looked so uneasy in the pink border, settled in happily among the peach flowers, I finally understood. A pink flower can be a cool, pinkish-blue, like sea thrift (*Armeria maritima*); or it can be warm, pinkish-orange like my pelargonium.

A big light bulb had just gone on in my head. It was a moment of revelation, comparable to the moment when I'd understood the importance of those plump, green pyrcanthas. In both cases, pictures of great gardens had first shown me what was possible to achieve. Then an accidental discovery in my own garden had given me a prod toward achieving it.

I saw now how I could improve several different areas

of my garden. For instance, I knew why the artichoke border I'd just planted was not quite finished, after all. Something about the color had been bothering me, and at last I knew why.

The flowers in the border were predominantly a light, bluish-purple. A few flowers, though, such as the 'Black Pearl' dahlia and the 'Sooty' sweet William were wine colored. I had mixed bluish-purple and reddish-purple flowers together under the mistaken impression that purple is purple is purple . . .

The only way to solve the problem was to move the reddish-purple flowers to the long back border, where the smokebush and the fountain grass already contributed a background of reddish-purple foliage. So that's what I did.

Using Color in a Small Garden

That fall, I read several books about color. One of them insisted that dark-leaved and dusky-flowered plants seem to recede, just as white flowers appear to leap forward. If that was true, I thought, the dark foliage at the back of the garden might give the space an illusion of extra depth. That certainly would be nice, though I wasn't sure if I believed that such tricks really worked. No games with color could completely camouflage the fact that I had a small garden.

The garden is so small, in fact, that the different areas bump up against each other without much transition. For example, the burgundy border curves into the peach border on one side and blends into the lavender-toned artichoke border on the other. To avoid clashing colors, I was careful to create a buffer of gray and green plants between the burgundies and the lavenders. On the north end, however, I let the peach flowers and burgundy foliage mingle a little, blurring the division between the two borders.

Another problem with a smallish garden is that more than one area shows at a time. If my property were larger, I might enclose the burgundy garden in curtains of neutral evergreens. Or I might build a long arbor to separate the

peach-colored garden from the pond garden. Then I would-
n't need to worry about the different areas clashing.

Of course, a person cannot look two ways at the same
time, that is one comfort. It's nearly impossible to see the
peach border and the lavender border simultaneously. Perhaps if you stood on a bench at the back of the deck you
could manage to see both at once, but you'd have to make
an effort.

You cannot, however, help viewing some sections of the
garden at once. Standing on the lawn, for example, your
gaze naturally passes from the pond to the back border. For
that reason, I tried to keep the long view in mind when I
fine-tuned my color scheme. I decided that the womb chamber and the bed around the pond should include mostly
pink flowers—not the warm peachy pinks of the left-hand
border, but cooler pinks. I knew the foreground of pink
flowers would complement the burgundy foliage and flowers behind it.

I also had to consider the view from the side of the pond,
taking in the womb chamber and the purple border beyond.
Luckily the pink flowers work in this situation, too. When
bits of lavender-purple show through here and there among
the pink plants, the effect is not thrilling, but it's not appal-
ling, either.

This garden-wide color scheme allows me to include a
range of colors in a fairly small space. Instead of limiting the
entire garden to hot or cool colors—either all reds, oranges,
and yellows or all blues and lavenders and pinks—I just
limited sections of the garden, keeping the views in mind
and making sure that each section of the garden complemented the sections near it.

This color scheme has helped me organize the garden,
although I've never let it rule me. I've left the clumps of blue
agapanthus and orange crocosmia in the peach border, bring-
ing intensity to a border that is primarily pale in color. And
at the other end, near the burgundy border, a spiky wine-red
New Zealand flax (*Phormium tenax* 'Rubrum') thrusts up

through the pale, peach blossoms on the 'Gruss an Aachen' rose bush. I've made exceptions in other places, too. For example, a few pink flowers bloom in the back border next to gray or burgundy foliage.

Of course, the color scheme continues to evolve, and I still make mistakes. Sometimes, I come home with a red flower that I could swear looked burgundy in the nursery. Or else I plant a flower that is too orange in the peach border, persuading myself that sunlight will fade its glaring tones. Occasionally, I panic. There are too many colors in the world, and I lack an artist's eye. But each year I grow more confident.

Progress

During those first few years, Paul used to say, "The garden doesn't seem to make you happy. You're always complaining about how terrible it looks. Why aren't you ever satisfied?"

He asked me this until I began to wonder if my chronic dissatisfaction could be a serious character flaw. Had I always been this hard to please?

Looking back, I realize that my garden peeved me so much not because I was especially critical but because the garden didn't match either the pictures in the books I'd read or the pictures in my head. Its never-ending awfulness frustrated me.

Gradually, my garden came to frustrate me less often because I improved it. I did not "mellow out." I did not "stop being so hard on myself." I did not lower my standards. I kept on fiddling with the design until I started to see more good things in it than bad.

Sometime during that fourth year, I began to see that my garden was improving. I was ecstatic. "Progress is not a fantasy," I said to myself. "Improvement is possible, if only on a small scale. And even if the moments of excellence fade quickly, they do at least exist."

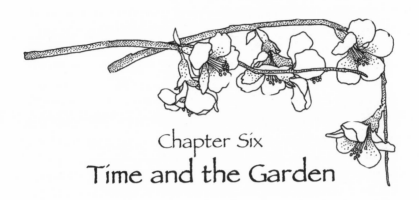

Chapter Six
Time and the Garden

The Garden Ripens—The Fifth Year

My newly reorganized garden looked bald for about a year. This baldness worried me. I looked at my skimpy borders, filled with wispy clumps of society garlic and scrub-shaped lavenders, and lamented that those sprouts would never be real plants. I didn't fully understand how much difference time would make. I should have calmed down and waited and had faith, but in a strange illogical way I didn't believe the plants would grow.

A change in my garden, however, occurred during the fifth year: at last, it stopped looking bare. Suddenly it seemed to burst with leaves and flowers. The plants grew tall and fat. Bare spaces filled in. And patchy, uncertain areas looked more settled.

These changes occurred rapidly. In fact, once the borders finally started to fill in, they improved so quickly that I felt I must have cheated somehow. I was so used to fussing and agonizing, weeding and worrying, that when at last my work began to pay off—I was astonished.

That astonishment, I'm happy to say, soon turned to pleasure. I began to take comfort in my garden's maturity. My years of association with my pepper tree, my peculiar lemon tree, my diminutive star magnolia gratified me. I thought to myself, "I've been tending these trees quite a few years, now . . ." I considered all the jars of quince chutney I'd given away at Christmas, I thought of the baskets of lemons I'd picked—and I felt rich. What was more important, I felt I had a history.

My garden was becoming my past. I felt secure. The large, ample shrubs and generous clumps of perennials seemed almost maternal. I buried myself in their laps, metaphorically. At the same time, I strutted around feeling extremely pleased with myself. After all, I had mothered the plants that now mothered me. I had tended all those frail fuchsia cuttings and small forlorn clumps of Japanese anemone from my mother's garden. Time, and the passing of seasons, had done a lot of the work, but I had helped foster the abundance. I still wasn't ready to consider actual motherhood but, for the first time, I began to take pleasure in nurturing, and to take pride in being responsible for other lives.

Camouflaging with Plants

One summer morning during that fifth year, I stood across the street and marveled at my vine-clad house. The yellow and white Lady Banks roses (*Rosa banksiae* and 'White Banksia') had finished blooming, but the fleece-vine (*Polygonum aubertii*) veiled the south corner of the house with long shaggy clusters of white flowers. A plumbago (*Plumbago auriculata*) spilling out of half a wine barrel in the driveway hid part of the south wall under sky-blue blossoms. And farther down the driveway, a tangle of passion vine (*Passiflora alatocaerulea*) curled up a lattice and wound around the kitchen windows. From where I stood across the street, the walls of my house hardly showed at all.

Unsightly garden features also disappeared under veils of foliage. For instance, the weathered fence on the side of the property supported a profusion of passion vine and star jasmine. And, of course, containers of vegetables and bright flowers covered most of the driveway.

I must have looked peculiar, standing there on the sidewalk, smiling smugly to myself. Passersby stared at me. They didn't realize that I was especially pleased with my flowery house because I knew its secret. I knew what an poor ugly thing the old building was under its new clothes. I knew that the roof tiles, under those white frothy blossoms, were beginning to curl. I knew that the window frames were aluminum and the shingles were asbestos.

Paul and I had talked about having those asbestos shingles removed when we first moved into the house. Then we discovered that the disposal of the hazardous waste would be extraordinarily expensive. So instead of remodelling, we decided to hide the whole house under petals and leaves. It was an easy, inexpensive solution, and very pretty.

That was why I looked so smug. I had discovered how much I could do with plants. I couldn't do a whole lot for the inside of my house. I couldn't grow a dining table. I couldn't grow a sofa. But outside I could do almost everything. I could plant some packets of seeds and I could help some small plants grow large, and in that way I could literally shape the outdoor environment. I could make a world.

No one could look at my house and say, "There is a tacky little place hidden under those plants," because the garden enveloped the house and gave it character. No one could judge the garden for having cheap parts, because the garden was more than a collection of plants and concrete and redwood boards. It was a lovely, harmonious whole. It radiated confidence, purpose, and rightness. The components no longer mattered.

At least that's what I thought to myself as I stood across the street, looking at my house in bloom. Tomorrow the roses might mildew or the fuchsias' leaves might curl up with mites again. Or I might decide that the iris were looking ratty and the jade plants should be moved. But for that one wonderful moment, the world I had created satisfied me.

Time and the Frugal Gardener

I was pleased that the passing years had made up for what I had been unable to buy. So what if those miniature hedges of candytuft had grown from cuttings, and the bergenia, clustered like a hundred ping-pong paddles around the base of the pepper tree, had multiplied out of a half-dozen plants from my mother's garden? So what if the voluptuous oriental poppies had come out of a six-pack and not out of five-gallon pots? It made no difference now.

Why do people think you have to be rich to garden, I wondered. All those teak benches and market umbrellas and gazing globes in the catalogs must have fooled them—as though gazing globes matter! Gardening with lots of money must be very nice. But I am proof that thrifty gardeners find their own special satisfactions.

Vanished

Time improved my garden, but the improvements were sometimes bittersweet. I had sacrificed some of my favorite plants as I refined the garden design. And when I walked in my garden in the fifth year, I saw their ghosts all around me.

I looked at the shady corner where the oakleaf hydrangea spread its wonderful leaves and remembered when a jumble of columbine and bleeding hearts bloomed there, filling the bare spaces around the immature shrub. I had prized those delicate woodland plants, with finely wrought blossoms quivering in the spring winds. Now I prized the big bold shrub that had crowded them out. Which "garden picture" was lovelier? I couldn't say.

I seldom felt more than a passing pang for most of the vanished plants, however. Instead, I found myself looking toward the future with interest and curiosity. In five years, my meadow of weeds had come a long way. I was dying to know what the next five years would bring.

During an alfresco breakfast one morning in July, Paul asked me, "Are you still anxious to move to up the hills?"

I was incredulous. Move? "Are you serious?" I asked. "Perhaps a bigger house would be nice. Perhaps a quieter neighborhood would be pleasant. But you know I can't leave. I have to stay here and see how the garden turns out."

And half-joking, I pounded my fist on the breakfast table and roared, "This garden is my *home*. I made it, damn it, and I'm not leaving until I can walk *under* the star magnolia." Then I added in my normal voice, "And since the star magnolia seems to be frozen at three and a half feet, we may have to live here for quite a while."

I didn't mind waiting. I was happy. I had settled in. I was like the passion vine twining over the redwood fence, making itself more at home in the garden every month. That vine was "established," as the gardening books say. And I was established, too.

Maintenance—The Sixth and Seventh Years

The next couple years were largely devoted to maintenance, which is never much fun. But weeding and deadheading are necessary, repetitive tasks, like washing dishes and cleaning the bathroom. Like most of us, I would always rather embark on a new project. I would rather remodel the living room than vacuum it again. And I would rather design a new border than groom an old one. But unlike a house, which ages badly, gathering dust and grime, the passing years improve a garden. At least I had the satisfaction of knowing that the borders I weeded in the seventh year were prettier than the borders I had weeded in the sixth year, or the fifth, or the fourth.

When I wasn't busy with routine chores, such as weeding, deadheading, spraying, pruning and spreading compost, I continued to move plants around, refining my design. And once in a while, I went on a binge at the local nursery and brought home a couple of shrubs or a few perennials. I always enjoyed learning about new plants.

Renovation—The Eighth Year

In the eighth year, an imposing chore lay ahead of me. My borders needed renovating—a thorough overhaul.

Or did they?

I wasn't sure. For months, I postponed making a decision. I didn't want to think about taking on such an enormous task. But the subject kept cropping up in the books I read.

One night in September, as I lay in bed flipping through a new gardening encyclopedia, I came upon a drawing of a man dividing a big wad of roots. He was performing the task the way people in gardening books always do—with two gardening forks held back to back.

I snorted to myself, "Does anyone really divide perennials that way? Do ordinary gardeners even *own* two gardening forks?" Then I read the text beneath the picture: "A mature border such as this one should be entirely renovated in its seventh or eighth year."

I sighed. There it was again. The subject I wished to avoid. I told myself I ought to make a decision one way or the other. It was September. Autumn was an excellent time for renovating borders. The question was, should I or shouldn't I?

I studied the page, reading an awesome description of how the author had dug the plants out of his eighty-foot border, divided the overcrowded ones, amended the soil, and put the new divisions back again.

"Isn't there any way to reduce the work?" I asked myself. "Must I dig out *all* the plants?" I read the page again, looking for loopholes.

I was relieved to see that the shrubs and trees could stay put. Succulents didn't require digging up either. Neither did annuals and biennials, naturally. In fact, as far as I could see, most of the "mixers" in a mixed border were allowed to remain in place.

"The author doesn't really mean that I should dig up everything," I decided, feeling encouraged. "He only means that I should divide the perennials."

Even there, I found a few more loopholes—for as I read further I found out that many perennials prefer to remain untouched. Some, such as Japanese anemones, need years to become established and do not appreciate being dug up just as they're getting comfortable. Others, such as plants with long taproots, including oriental poppies and baptisia, also are happier left alone. So what was left?

I lay back in bed picturing the clump-forming perennials in my own garden. Many of them I had recently dug up, moving them around as part of my gardening musical chairs. And I had taken the opportunity to divide them while they were out of the ground, for as usual, I was greedy for more plants.

That left me with about six or seven clump-forming perennials that just might need dividing. I would take a look tomorrow. Perhaps I would find that all seven clumps needed dividing, but I doubted it. More likely, a couple of them would be overgrown, one would be in its prime, and the rest would still be on the small side. After all, perennials don't all mature at an even rate, I reasoned. I bent over the book once more, to see if I really needed to revamp my borders, after all.

Apparently dividing the plants was only one of the reasons. The book stressed that the eighth year was also the time to refine the borders' design, to set all the little plants neatly into their balloon-shaped drifts and masses, to tidy up, to get back to the early days when the plantings were as neat as a paint-by-numbers canvas. But my raw young borders never had been tidy. Well maybe they'd been tidy, briefly, but they'd surely not been beautiful. And beauty really was the object, after all.

I was pretty sure that digging up my plants and starting again with a graph-paper design would be a mistake. I already knew that I couldn't work on graph-paper. I was no good at that kind of gardening. And working with little stubby plants on patches of bare dirt was not much easier. Not when it was such a big, once-every-eight-years production. The prospect terrified me. I liked to shift plants around on an almost daily basis, keeping the trees and shrubs as a sort of framework. I liked the borders to evolve slowly.

The way I worked now, there were always just-planted spots here and there, and other sections of mature plants that usually made up for the bare zones. I couldn't see the point of renovating an entire border all at once, because afterwards the area would look bald again. I had waited years for my plants to grow up. I didn't want to start all over.

After some thought, I felt free to ignore the book's recommendation. "My plants do *not* need replanting," I said. "They've already been moved quite enough, lately. If anything, they need a rest."

But one more detail nagged at me. What about rejuvenating the soil?

According to the book, this was the time to dig deeply into the soil—two or three feet, the book said—and add fertilizer. But this didn't seem necessary, either. I always added compost whenever I moved a plant or replaced a dead one or divided an overgrown clump. And of course I mulched with more compost. Because the fertility of the soil in my garden improved a little every day, I didn't need to make a big production of incorporating tons of fertilizer all at once.

"Thank goodness," I said, slapping the book closed and setting it down on the floor. I couldn't help thinking that the author of that particular gardening book must still be living in the age of estates and hired help. How do other, ordinary gardeners tend their mature borders, I wondered. As far as I knew, my mother had never dug up a border in her life. Perhaps, though, she wasn't the best role model, for her garden was a jungle of overgrown plants.

I would have enjoyed discussing my garden's growing pains with a knowledgeable, seasoned gardener from down the street. But that was only a fantasy. I didn't know any gardeners in my neighborhood. In this matter—as in so many others—I had to find my own way.

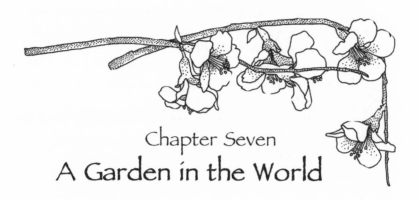

Chapter Seven
A Garden in the World

Our Ninth Spring in the Neighborhood

As the years passed, I found myself wishing more and more often that I knew other gardeners in my neighborhood. But I was starting to realize that I didn't live in a community of garden makers. When I ran into my Berkeley neighbors on the sidewalk, we chatted about the weather, politics, potholes in the street, cats, dogs, kids, cars—never about our gardens.

On bright Saturday mornings in spring, I occasionally spotted a few of my neighbors walking home from the local nursery with six-packs of snapdragons, or perhaps big Transvaal daisies in four inch pots. Something in the spring air made these people want to plant. The majority of my neighbors, though, were immune to spring air; flowers didn't seem to interest them.

Apparently this hadn't always been the case. Here and there around the neighborhood I saw ghosts of former gardens. Sometimes I walked around the streets near my house like a detective searching for these remains. In one yard, I saw hundreds of cream-colored freesias blooming above a disarray of grassy weeds. In another untended plot, I spotted *vinca minor* crawling over the cracked, dead-looking earth and blooming a heavenly blue.

Most of the surviving plants grew in neglected yards, but here and there they persisted in re-done gardens. These were the rebels. In one garden, a solitary iris—a yellow Dutch iris—bloomed cheerfully in the middle of a desert of glittering white gravel. In another yard, scores of pumpkin-orange sparaxis popped out of a tidy blanket of prostrate juniper. Funny how the surviving flowers were invariably bright. Insolently bright. True nonconformists.

I suspected that the current garden owner had not known the sparaxis were there when he planted his conservative, low-maintenance garden of junipers. Who had knelt in the dirt long ago to plant those corms, I wondered. I also wondered how many of my own plants would survive if I moved away.

Probably scale would kill the star jasmine, I thought. Mites would get the fuchsias if I stopped spraying them with oil, and the iris would overcrowd, eventually. The roses would stop blooming if no one deadheaded them. The bulbs would dwindle, but the corms would multiply. The freesias and sparaxis and ixia would most likely survive. They're probably the most self-sufficient plants in the garden.

Then I realized that the blackberries would thrive, too. Morning glory would take over and the calla lilies would grow out of bounds again. I imagined my abandoned garden too clearly, and terrified myself with the vision.

Temptation

My immediate neighbors, to the north, south, and east, were no different from most of the people in the neighborhood. Like almost everyone else, they were content to let their back yards become wildernesses. Sometimes, though, the abundance of plant life and bug life that thrived in those back yards threatened my own garden, provoking a moral dilemma.

I never had much difficulty gardening organically—in my own garden, that is. The healthy plants usually remained free of bugs. I pulled weeds by hand and collected all the snails I could find. But what about the bugs and snails and weeds that came in from next door? At times, I felt a strong urge to unleash all the destructive power of Ortho on my neighbors.

I grew so sick of cutting back morning glories that I wanted to get up on a ladder and spray RoundUp over the fence into the jungles next door. And I wanted—sometimes desperately!—to sprinkle poison pellets over the fence into the dark, dense vines where the snails bred. For I knew that the sneaky mollusks slept there during the day, making forays into my yard by night.

But I knew just as clearly that any poison pellets I threw over the fence would kill worms as well as snails. (I had seen dead worms among the snail corpses in my mother's garden.) And I did not want to kill worms in *anyone's* garden. So I resisted the temptation to poison those bothersome snails.

Glorious Weather and Dismal Gardens

From time to time, I asked myself why so few of my neighbors seem to garden. Maybe because the weather is too fine, seemed to be the answer. Maybe gardening is not challenging enough in California. Maybe people need to contend with hurricanes and floods and ten feet of snow before they decide to plant mixed borders.

In my readings during that ninth year, I came across stories about dedicated cold-weather gardeners on the East Coast or in the rocky mountain states. "They are the *real* gardeners," I told Paul, waving my book at him. "And so are the southwestern gardeners who deal with dry heat, southeastern gardeners who cope with wet heat, and northwestern gardeners who cope with just plain *wet*."

"I'd still rather live in California," Paul said.

I wasn't so sure. Individually, those determined, hard-working gardeners created lovely landscapes. And together they formed communities of gardeners. I envied that sense of fellowship.

Gardening books and magazines linked me to other gardeners, but sometimes I longed for real camaraderie. Paul suggested that I join a club, but all the clubs I had heard of celebrated single plants—daylilies or hydrangeas or dahlias—and I wasn't a collector. I cared more about garden design. Anyhow, I wasn't solemn enough about plants to join a club. I simply wished to chat with my neighbors; to gab about trivial things, such as how the clematis was doing or whether the spittle bugs were bad again this year.

But since I couldn't chat with my neighbors, I continued to get my gardening gossip from books. I read books describing gardeners in other parts of the country competing together to produce the first ripe tomato of the season, or the biggest dahlia blossom, or the most perfect long-stemmed rose. I could hardly believe the accounts. Nobody competed with me—that I knew of, anyhow. My neighbors never seemed to look at my garden, or take any interest in it, at all.

In some books, I read stories of people taking a bit too much interest in their neighbors' gardens. I read that nosy neighbors sometimes objected to front-yard wildflower gardens or vegetable beds in place of the traditional lawn. This news astonished me, and reminded me that my neighbors, even if they weren't gardeners, did possess some good characteristics—and tolerance was certainly one of them.

All kinds of 'gardens' (if you could call them gardens) existed in my neighborhood and no one ever objected to any of them. Some gardens bristled with political banners. One was wall-to-wall cannas in every color. Another inexplicably mixed cacti and gladioli. Several front yards looked like used-car lots. Several others had lovely vegetable plots, taking advantage of the western exposure. And some grew nothing at all—only sneaky crops of weeds under sheets of black plastic or areas of raked gravel.

With all this rampant individuality, I couldn't imagine anyone objecting to anything I might do to my front yard. I could cover it with astroturf and grow poison oak in urns and no one would say a word.

Reaching Out

My neighbors' indifference nonetheless amazed me. How could they not notice my front yard? It was positively flamboyant. Aloe, spider plants, agapanthus, fuchsias, plumbago, abutilon, ferns, Japanese anemone, and roses—especially roses—jostled each other, all demanding attention. The roses climbed the house, climbed the trees, even climbed into the telephone wires and stretched out toward the street. The front yard seemed to shout, "Look at me!" At the height of the season, when the garden spilled over with bloom, it almost embarrassed me.

In April of the ninth year, Paul built a fence to contain the abundance. He made the fence low and slatted, vaguely California "craftsman" style, like our house. On rainy days, when I sat reading on the living room sofa, feeling stir-crazy, the slats looked like prison bars. They seem to separate me from the rest of the world, to hold me in.

But the fence couldn't hold my garden in. The ferns leaned through the bars, the clumps of hen-and-chicks bulged over the sidewalk. The 'Cecile Brunner' rose on the north side of the garden reached up over the fence, trailing thorny fingers across the scalps of passersby.

I chopped the rambling rose back almost weekly, but all the same, once as I was getting into my car a young woman stopped me on the curb to tell me that every morning as she hurried to work she risked putting her eye out on my rose. She made me feel like the owner of a big sloppy overly affectionate dog. I wanted to assure her that my plants wouldn't hurt her. They only reached out because they were friendly.

Sometimes packs of girls from the junior high school tore flowers from the rose bushes by the sidewalk. If they glimpsed me watching from the living room window they would flee, laughing and shrieking, holding the flowers up to their noses. Actually, I didn't mind their pilfering. I was flattered. I only wished they would learn to break off the flowers at an outward facing leaf bud above a cluster of five leaves.

A Gathering Place

Since my garden couldn't go out into the world (although the 'Cecile Brunner' rose was trying) I decided to invite the world into my garden. Or at least, some of it.

This was a big change for Paul and me. We always had considered the garden our private place. The very first time we carried the dining table out to the deck and ate a meal there, looking out over our wine glasses at a sea of onion grass and nasturtiums, the yard inside the six-foot wooden fence felt like a sanctuary, a retreat from the world. And we liked it that way.

Even after I pulled out the weeds and filled the space with plants, we seldom invited people into our little oasis. At that time, we were still adolescents, really, and we liked to go to other people's parties and enjoy the free food and drink. We could not yet imagine ourselves as hosts.

As the garden matured, however, we matured too. Although we still thought of our garden as our secret sanctuary, by the ninth year we decided we would like to share that secret.

At first, inviting other people into the garden made me anxious. They wouldn't understand that daylilies always look unkempt after they bloom. They wouldn't realize that oriental poppies always die down in July. They would think my flowers were sick; they would think I was a bad gardener.

I shouldn't have worried: our families and friends turned out to be horticulturally indifferent. Not only did they never mistake floppy plants for unhealthy plants, they never even noticed which ones were genuinely ill—those that were discolored or were crawling with aphids. Of course, they also didn't judge my skills as a gardener. They never flinched at the 'Pride-'n-Joy' roses with their apricot-flame blooms just inches from a violet-colored iris. They never sneered at the morning glory vines tangling in the plum trees or told me that the snow-in-summer needed shearing back. And when the bachelor's buttons flopped forward onto the lawn, they just stepped right over them.

Instead, *I* was the critical one. In the middle of our first party, I wanted to run into the greenhouse for stakes and twine. I wanted to fetch the clippers. During a conversation with Paul's brother, I found myself studying a long thread of bindweed in a border ten feet away, following it with my eyes, inch by inch, up a rose bush. My fingers twitched. I longed to run over there and yank it out. But instead, I held my paper plate primly and smiled at Paul's brother.

For the most part, I appreciated my guests' easygoing indifference. But sometimes I would have welcomed a few words about my garden. Eventually, I realized that one of the reasons our friends never criticized the garden was that they didn't think of it as a place I had made, a place I was still in the process of making. It just *was*. The lawn was a carpet, the borders of flowers walls, the entire garden an out-door room. It was all a pleasant blur to them.

Sometimes during those parties, a wild urge rose up in me. I wanted to make them see my garden. I wanted to draw their attention to corners they might have missed, to color schemes they might not have noticed, or interesting textures they certainly had not observed. But I restrained myself.

Except with Paul. I bothered him terribly. Especially about the foxgloves. Those lovely foxgloves. I was awful about the foxgloves.

I said, "Look at those apricot foxgloves blooming behind the salmon yarrow. Aren't they stunning?"

"Oh yes," he said. "I've seen them."

"You may have *seen* them, but you haven't *looked* at them," I said.

He smiled at me, slightly puzzled. "They're pretty, but what's the big deal, anyway? They were there last year, weren't they?"

"Those were different foxgloves!" I shouted. And I jumped up and down with frustration as I tried to explain to him about biennials. And then I marched him over to the greenhouse and showed him the row of four-inch pots with a little green rosette in the middle of each one. "Those are next year's foxgloves. And when you see them blooming behind the salmon yarrow next April you'd better not think they were there this year!"

Paul looked at me as though he felt sorry for me. "What's the matter? I thought you liked gardening," he said. "You shouldn't do it if causes you so much stress."

I realized then that I'd come close to spoiling the apricot foxgloves. And they were such enchanting flowers, I didn't want to do that. So I shut up about them.

But I didn't stop thinking about them. Sometimes at parties, I felt like whispering fiercely to my foxgloves or roses or hollyhocks or even to a modest clump of succulents, "I appreciate you . . ." Like a lover, I flirted with my plants from across the lawn. Or I wandered over casually and brushed against them. "I see you, and I touch you. I know you, really know you," murmured the passionate voice in my head.

Nongardeners couldn't possibly understand how much work I put into those beds and borders—even if I occasionally missed a strand of bindweed. At brunch once, Paul's stepmother said, "Look at the way that fuchsia sprouted up among those ferns. I didn't know they grew wild around here."

My eyes must have bugged out of my head, but again I smiled primly. What's more I did not tell the whole, step-by-step story of that fuchsia—how I had clipped a branch from a shrub down the street, rooted the cutting, planted it out and pruned it and showered it with fish emulsion. I thought about everything I'd done just so those pale pink ballet-dancer blossoms would hover in just that delicate manner between the green swords of fern. Then I remembered the foxglove, and kept quiet. I let Paul's stepmother and all the rest of them go on imagining that the flowers in my garden grew by themselves. To a certain extent, they did.

If people took my garden for granted, it was my fault for deliberately designing a casual, relaxed landscape. I could have planted rows of plants that shouted out, "This is a garden!" Then maybe I would have received a little praise from my family. But I didn't want an intimidating garden or an impressive garden. I didn't even want a strictly formal garden. I only wanted a garden organized and regular enough to seem satisfying, to somehow look right.

I suppose I should have been proud that I'd created a garden with a design so natural, so inevitable that people assumed it all "came that way."

Of course if they'd been gardeners themselves they would have seen the flaws that winked at me from every garden corner. They would have offered their criticism and observations, and I might have liked that. Instead, they sometimes said vague, nice things. But most of all they flattered me incredibly by saying absolutely nothing—by merely wanting to be there.

Paul's mother, for instance, never kept a plant alive in her own garden for more than a month and never mourned their deaths, but despite her black thumb, she seemed to love my garden. If I asked her what she liked about the place, she probably wouldn't have been able to tell me. She clearly didn't notice color combinations or architectural foliage or interesting textures, at least not consciously. All the same, she lingered in my garden as though the place bewitched her.

I remember an Indian summer afternoon, about four months before I got pregnant. We had invited Paul's family over for a barbecue and the party was essentially over, but everyone still sat around, lazily. All the food was gone. The charcoal briquettes had turned powder-white, red-hot inside. "Look at the charcoal. We should have waited until now to start the meat," someone inevitably said. And other lazy voices spoke out, agreeing, laughing.

My brothers- and sisters-in-law lay on the lawn, beer bottles balanced on their chests, letting the sun flicker down on their closed eyelids through the leaves of the quince tree. Paul's mother and her boyfriend sat in chairs on the deck and cradled their wine glasses in their hands.

It was a normal Sunday afternoon, quiet, but not too quiet. We could smell other barbecues in other yards. My neighbor was practicing his oboe.

A blimp passed overhead, and we all looked up, trying to read the advertisement printed on its belly. We felt comfortable there in the garden, with the city around us.

I was pleased that nobody stirred to leave, flattered that they wanted to stay in my garden and watch the dusk fall. At that instant I didn't care that no one but I had noticed the way the silky black flowers of the tall hollyhocks (*Alcea rosea* 'Nigra') brought out the tiny black speckles on the white-flowered *Nemophila atomaria* 'Snowstorm,' that frothed around the hollyhocks' ankles. For once, I forgot about the details and sat back with half-closed eyes to enjoy the garden as a seamless whole—a place I had created.

I told myself that I was giving the garden—or at least those hours in the garden—to Paul's relatives as a very personal gift. And I enjoyed the idea that the giving was reciprocal, for as I took them into my garden, they took me into their family.

If I have a baby, they will be my baby's family, I thought then. I lay down on the cool grass with my head on Paul's lap, and I looked up into the sky and watched the sunset golds and pinks reflect off the big, slow metallic-colored blimp.

For the last six months, Paul and I had been talking about starting a family. We had joked about it, and we also had conversed seriously. We even had talked details. Our dresser could serve as a changing table, we told each other. The pond, emptied, would make a wonderful sandbox.

But still, I wasn't sure.

The world seemed precarious. Life seemed uncertain. When I sat in the back yard sometimes, the sound of birdsong was interrupted by the clatter of a shopping cart rattling down the sidewalk and the clank of bottles falling into the cart. All around me the garden was screaming out its absurd impractical almost decadent beauty, and out on the street a homeless person was going through our recycling, looking for bottles to redeem for cash.

The sound of the shopping cart always made me feel guilty, and also afraid.

I no longer yearned to live in a larger house or in a different neighborhood. I only worried that some disaster might force Paul and me to leave the place we had now. I imagined lost jobs, sickness, or accidents. These days, we couldn't count on being upwardly mobile. In fact, from all I had seen and heard, my generation seemed to be downwardly mobile. Yet a home and garden and a family required stability and money and time.

That autumn day, though, as I lay on the grass watching the blimp go by, I decided it was time to stop waiting and being afraid. Gardening had taught me that time passes, seasons go by, things change. If you wait too long, sometimes it's too late.

A few months after the day of the blimp, we conceived Leo.

Chapter Eight
Winter Rituals

The Tenth Year—A Specimen Year

Of all the years I have gardened, the tenth year—the year I was pregnant—stands out as the most memorable, even though nothing unusual happened, horticulturally speaking. Because I was pregnant, I felt the wheel of the year turn as I never had before. I seemed linked to the seasons in a new way. As the spring borders filled out, I filled out. And in Autumn, as the quinces in the quince tree grew large and heavy, the baby inside of me grew large and heavy, too.

Virginia Woolf used to write in her diary about specimen days. A specimen day is a typical day, without any extraordinary events to distinguish it from other days. A specimen day is usually a good day, in an ordinary sort of way. In fact, it is a good day just because it is so ordinary.

The year I was pregnant was a kind of specimen year— a year without any spectacular events, but a good year, nevertheless.

I did not have the energy or the money to add new features to the garden, so instead of launching projects I simply watched the seasons unfold and enjoyed their rhythm. I spread compost when the compost was ready to be spread.

I pruned the fuchsias at fuchsia-pruning time. And I planted the summer annuals at seed-planting time. I enjoyed those seasonal rituals almost as much as I enjoyed the succession of flowers that bloomed throughout the year. During my pregnancy, I was less obsessed with results and more involved in the daily act of gardening.

Of course, the specimen year included bleak times, as every year does. And because I was pregnant the bleak times occasionally felt grim. Winter depressed me more than usual that year. But I bounced back as soon as the weather improved, feeling the season's glory more keenly than I ever had before.

Conception

The first serious storm of the season came shortly after the new year. When it hit, Paul and I rushed outside to carry our dining table back into the house. After that, we ate our meals in the kitchen instead of on the deck. Paul didn't mind relocating, but I did. I missed the garden.

During those rainy days, I often stood at the kitchen window, looking out at the back yard through the steamy glass. Those were the first days of my pregnancy when I was too newly pregnant to be absolutely sure of my condition. I had to wait, and waiting made me restless. Luckily, I found a strange comfort in a landscape that seemed as restless and unsettled as I was.

The garden was not dormant and serene as wintery landscapes usually are. A handful of hard-working perennials still slogged on through the cold wet weather. In the peach border, a rose with mildewed stems and speckled petals blossomed near a stunted calla lily. Near the driveway, a clump of Shasta daisies waved undersized flowers on the ends of long, weak stems. Around the womb chamber, clusters of soggy pink yarrow hung on bent stalks. A pelargonium lay face down in the mud. A deluded iris flowered on a painfully short stalk. And an odd-looking oriental poppy bloomed on no stalk at all.

A Snowy Garden

In some parts of the country, I knew, of course, plants doze through the winter under a carpet of snow. I wasn't familiar with cold weather gardening, but I remembered visiting my aunt's snowy Connecticut garden once when I was a teenager. It was a garden utterly unlike the disheveled yard my parents and I had left it behind in California. It looked clean and handsome, the bones of its landscape—the fences and trees and paths—standing out strongly through a sheet of white. And of course no sickly, depressing flowers marred the scene.

The snowy garden was like a canvas on which my aunt painted dreamy pictures of the spring to come. I remember her and my mother sitting together on the sofa, leafing through plant catalogs bright with photographs of delphiniums, lupines, and peonies.

"Can you really grow all these flowers here?" my mother asked jealously. Her own peony back home in Berkeley never bloomed.

In answer, my aunt gestured out the window at the wonderful blank whiteness and described lush, immaculate borders bursting with dazzling flowers and luxuriant foliage. Inspired (and perhaps deluded) by those gorgeous catalogs, my aunt projected a fantasy garden onto the frosty yard. And my mother and I believed in her fantasy.

Years later, I envied my aunt her season of dreams. When I looked at my winter garden during that long rainy January, I saw a real place, not a fantasy. The yard outside my kitchen window begged to be raked and weeded. Debris from the storms littered the lawn. Weeds crowded the borders.

I thought of my aunt saying, "Weeds can't grow in snow-covered borders. When the snow comes, the garden gets to rest and I get to rest, too." I sighed, knowing that no blanket of snow was likely to cover the eyesores in *my* garden. Only hard work would eliminate them.

Getting Dirty

One morning toward the end of the month, I woke to find that the wind had blown the clouds away during the night. I was glad to see blue sky again. As soon as I was dressed, I cracked open the kitchen door and stepped off the deck onto the long, wet grass.

My garden looked terrible. It seemed to be nothing more than a collection of homely plants, one next to the other—thump, thump, thump—with a lot of mud and weeds in between. I could hardly believe that the garden would ever look pretty again, with its plants filling out and blending together.

The recent rains had brought up a crop of onion grass and sour grass, and had sent the wild violets running their tough, knotty roots through all the borders. Bright yellow dandelions bloomed in the mud near the deck, too.

But while the weeds were obviously thriving, the culti-vated plants did not seem to be enjoying the wet weather. The drought-loving plants looked positively soggy. The gray-leaved perennials, such as lamb's ears and lavender, were starting to turn Irish-green—a sickening color in plants usu-ally reminiscent of dusty mediterranean hills. A few more weeks of rain and the sodden plants would start to rot.

Other plants didn't seem to mind the rain so much, but suffered from the cold. A light frost had scorched the tips of the spider plants, wilted the nasturtiums, and reduced the round, fleshy, wax begonias to spare, brown fingers point-ing out of the earth.

I stomped over to one of the disfigured begonias and kicked it rudely with my boot. I half-wished the thing would die and get it over with. But I knew it wouldn't. Unless one of our rare January freezes struck, all the tender plants would flirt with death without ever quite succumbing. For the plants' safety, I would have to wait until the weather warmed to cut away the damaged parts. Then the plants would start to recover. They would grow back from their bases, and by March they would be fine. Until then, they would keep my garden looking ugly as sin.

I could do nothing yet to improve the unsightly perennials, but at least I could get rid of the weeds. Anxious to do *something*, I went off to the greenhouse to fetch my clippers, a trowel, and an empty bucket to hold the weeds.

As I crossed the lawn, a light drizzle began to fall. The sky darkened and Paul turned on the kitchen lights inside the house. I could see him in the bright window, staring at me. No doubt he wondered why I was standing in the rain. He gestured at me, but I ignored him. I couldn't go inside just yet. The garden called to me.

I crouched down near a patch of dandelions. The leaves were wet against my hand. I worked my fingers under the green rosette. I grasped, I twisted, I tugged. And the long root popped out.

"One down and five to go," I thought. But I hesitated for a moment before continuing. Trapped indoors for weeks, I had grown soft—finicky and fastidious and no longer used to the sensation of gardening. The mud around the plant felt very sticky on my clean fingers. The leaves felt prickly. The rainwater on the leaves felt cold.

Part of me recoiled from the textures and sensations of the wet plants and mud and stones and twigs, from the prickly things and slimly things and cold things. I was still warm and dry, inside my coat. I carried an aura of indoors around me. I had not quite disengaged myself from the cozy warm house. I had not broken that shell.

I waited for a moment before going on. Then the urge to get more dandelions prevailed and I started to work seriously, enthusiastically.

So that was that. Rain fell and the bucket beside me filled with water as well as weeds. I had gone from being a dry indoor person to being a muddy wet outdoor person. I had plunged in and I didn't want to go back. I was an animal of the outdoors, now. The house seemed foreign and far away, and I was glad. To be dry and cozy was nice, but the touch of the wet earth was something different, something irresistible.

I knew then that I could never bear to live in a snowy part of the country. Though I could see the advantage of a winter break from all the gardening chores, I wouldn't appreciate the rest. I would miss the garden too intensely— yes, even the weeds and the mud. After all, if a short rainstorm reduced me to a caged, pacing animal, what would four months of snow and frozen earth do to me? I would start rooting around in the house plants, just to remind myself of the feeling of dirt on my hands.

As I crouched there on the wet grass, I realized that I truly am a California gardener. I'm like one of those out-of-season perennials—the stunted calla lily or the stemless poppy. I don't know how to rest, and more than that, I don't really want to rest.

Springtime—Sort Of

A week passed before I had a chance to walk through the garden again, and in that time the garden changed. It entered an in-between stage. Winter ended but spring hung back, as if unwilling to take its place.

The garden looked indefinite; neither one thing nor the other. Big furry fawn-colored buds decorated the star magnolia in the womb chamber while small and scaly green buds bulged along the branches of the espaliered fruit trees in the purple border. Those buds pointed forward to the blooms of March. At the same time, though, the bedraggled perennials in the border around the trees pointed backward to the storms of early January.

I was at an in-between stage, too—for at that time I was still waiting to find out whether or not I was pregnant. I wanted the days to pass quickly, to the time when I would know for sure. If I could find proof that winter was ending, then I would feel more certain that my own time of waiting was almost over, too. So I wandered through the garden, searching for evidence of spring.

And I found some. Along the edges of the pond, I saw nubs of daffodil leaves poking out of the ground, and in the purple border, I discovered the pointy green foliage belonging to half a dozen 'Queen of the Night' tulips. Then, in the peach border, I found a cluster of thick, knobby hyacinths nudging aside the wet leaves beneath the quince tree.

With a burst of affection, I stooped down to pat the firm, plasticky buds. The largest one already showed hints of white. Within a week, it would be in bloom. I bent down further until my nose touched the wet tip. Unfortunately, no perfume came from the flower yet.

Feeling slightly let down, I stood and scanned the garden. The sun told me that I had come looking for spring too soon. It was still a winter sun, harsh and bleak—not mild, like a springtime sun. It picked out every imperfection in the garden. Beneath its glare, the tufts of grass stood out, edged in black; the scattered leaves on the lawn cast hard little shadows.

I looked up at the branches of the quince tree overhead, but saw no signs of spring there either. No leaf buds. No flower buds.

I told myself, "When those bare branches flower, I'll know for certain whether or not I'm pregnant. And when the branches sag with yellow fruit, I will—quite possibly—give birth."

I stared at the tree for a long time, thinking of what I'd told myself. Time and the passing of seasons seemed incredible. The garden around me was so physical, so solid, so real—I could hardly believe it would ever change.

Hyacinths

A few hours later, rain began to fall once more, and fell, off and on, for several days. When I went outside again, I discovered that spring had come a bit closer.

The hyacinths were in bloom now. Chalk-white flowers rose among brown, rust-red, and rain-blackened leaves. The sight of last year's leaves plastered down next to the first flowers of the new year reminded me of how quickly winter passes in California. It had seemed interminable that year, but I could see that it hadn't really been long at all—not even long enough for autumn's leaves to decompose.

At last, I began to feel that the irritating in-between-stage would also end soon. Already spring seemed closer.

Crocuses

The most dramatic addition to the scene was a clump of silky purple crocuses blooming in a patch of wooly gray snow-in-summer beneath the row of 'Iceberg' roses by the deck. The flowers looked like tiny hot air balloons.

In West Coast gardens, crocuses are extremely ephemeral flowers, lasting only a day or two. If the rain hadn't let up that morning, I might have missed them entirely. They might have bloomed and faded away, unseen.

Already a few of them lay deflated on their sides— yesterday's blooms. Those withered crocuses were the first spent flowers of the season. It was exciting to think about how many more flowers would bloom and fade before the year was over. When I looked at those small purple flowers —the dead ones, the full-blown ones, and the furled buds still half-hidden in the bladelike foliage—I saw the year unfolding. That single clump of flowers seemed to encompass the past, the present, and the future. The crocuses told me that the year was beginning—and also that it would, eventually, end.

In Quince-Blossom Time

Two weeks later, the fruit trees flowered, decorating the wintry garden with their charming, almost frivolous, blossoms.

Only a short while ago, the garden had confined its stirrings of life to tiny greenish-red leaf buds and the blades of emerging daffodils. Now, it consented to be less subtle. *I* had been able tell that spring was coming in January. But now, in early February, even Paul could look out the kitchen window at the flowering trees and say, "I guess winter's almost over."

The nectarines and plums were showiest. They bloomed on leafless branches, their flowers transforming the twigs into candy-colored pipe cleaners. Nonetheless, I preferred the quince's subtler beauty.

Unlike the other fruit trees, the quince had leafed out already. Its pale green leaves hung down from the branches, while the flowers faced upward, like tiny cups. During those weeks of bloom, I often stood beneath the quince tree's branches and looked up at the pale pink flowers fixed against the intensely blue spring sky.

Back in rainy January, I had told myself that by the time the quince tree bloomed I would know whether or not I was pregnant. Sure enough, during quince-blossom time, I found out that I was indeed expecting a baby.

Sprouts

Though the signs of spring lifted my spirits, I had to admit that the season was not entirely attractive. The garden did not leap into beauty all at once. Slivers of loveliness glinted out at me from the borders as the early daffodils joined the crocuses and hyacinths, and the calla lilies began to bloom in earnest. The great bulk of the garden, however, continued to look drab. Most of the perennials in my garden were evergreen, and after a hard winter the evergreen plants were shabby.

I knew that spring arrived differently in other parts of the country. An account I had read of a garden in Vermont included several lyrical descriptions of fragile, green shoots piercing black earth. Spring in my garden was less theatrical. I had to make do with the sight of small fine feathery leaves rising from the base of a ratty yarrow plant.

A few perennials in my garden, though, did die down in the winter. And when they rose from the earth, they were as fresh and new as the sprouts in the book about Vermont. But while they were dormant, those plants worried me. I was so unused to plants dying down to the ground that I half-suspected the ones that did were down for good.

Sedum spectabile 'Brilliant,' in the purple border, was one of those worrisome plants, but at least it didn't remain dormant for very long. Shortly after the old stalks keeled over, little rosettes appeared just above the soil level. The rosettes were like miniature versions of the full sized plants. They seemed to contain the future within them. When I looked at them, I could almost see the clumps of sedum telescoping upward. So I didn't worry too much about the sedum.

Nor did I fret much about the coneflowers (*Echinacea purpurea* 'Bravado'), also in the purple border, for they also sent up little tufts almost as soon as they died down.

I also wasn't too concerned about the dormant bulbs and corms, because even in an idle state, they seemed tough enough to take care of themselves. A few times, I accidently dug up some sparaxis corms, but I always reburied them and never felt guilty. They could weather the rough treatment, I felt sure.

I did worry, though, about my six clumps of *Geranium* 'Johnson's Blue,' in the front yard. In early February, the earth where they ought to have been was still bare. In all the borders, leaves were unfurling and buds were forming. Signs of the coming spring were everywhere. But in that one section of the border, by the sidewalk, winter seemed to linger.

I couldn't help thinking that the geraniums were dead. During a light frost in December, I remembered, they had behaved exactly like dying plants: the leaves had gone black and mushy; the stems had turned to straw. Eventually, there had been nothing left of the plants at all.

In February, I paced up and down the strip of sodden Bermuda grass, looking at the bare spots in the border where the plants ought to have been. I reminded myself that the roots under the soil were probably strong and sound, but I didn't really believe it. I doubted that the plants would ever sprout again.

I knew I ought to have faith and wait and be patient—
but I was getting sick of waiting and hoping. My mood was
as sullen as the gray sky. When I visited my doctor for my
monthly check up, I eyed all the other, more obviously pregnant women in the waiting room. I'm pregnant, I told myself, so how come I don't feel pregnant? When I got home,
I eyed those bald spots in the border. Nothing was happening to the geraniums. Nothing was happening to me. Those
tardy plants heightened my own sense of stagnation.

Then one day I discovered a greenish-red tendril sprawl-
ed on the soil where yesterday I had seen only mud. "It's
alive!" I said. Two more plants appeared overnight. The next
morning, another.

That evening, I walked along the edge of the border,
moving my lips as though in prayer. I was counting, "One,
two, three . . . weren't there four this morning?" I bent
down for a closer look, searching frantically, hoping a snail
hadn't got it. "Four, what a relief." I had forgotten that it
grew so close to the 'Cecile Brunner' rose bush.

In the end, five out of the six geraniums returned. When
the five plants were large, I dug in the dirt where the sixth
should have been. I found nothing. All the roots were gone.
Why? I wondered. Where had the plant gone? Why had
that one died, instead of the others?

I was glad the geraniums had returned, but my worries
weren't over yet. Now that I was no longer plagued by the
missing geraniums, I began to fret about a daylily I had
severed with my shovel while setting out some lobelia seedlings. "I forgot it was there!" I complained to Paul, showing him a hunk of amputated root. "It will never come back,
now. I've probably killed it."

I agonized over that plant so much that I almost began
to hate it. Why did it have to die down to the ground, anyway? Why couldn't it be sensibly evergreen, like the coreopsis or the penstemon?

I should have saved my concern for a more vulnerable
plant. That daylily turned out to be bursting with robust life.
When it eventually sprouted, it broke through the ground

with astonishing vigor, the entire clump rising out of the ground at once—more like an elevator than a plant.

I took Paul out to the border so that he could admire it, too. We crouched down together and ran our hands over the daylily's mat of thick, curving leaves. Paul was as pleased as I was to see evidence of such powerful life. We told ourselves that our baby would grow as sturdily and inexorably as that sturdy plant.

Regarding Leaves

In February, my garden was a jumble of new growth, old storm-damaged plants, and flashes of beauty that never seemed to last very long. A perky yellow primrose bloomed beside a nasturtium vine that had collapsed from cold. Crocuses bloomed and faded rapidly. A gust of wind sent showers of pink petals out of the nectarine tree.

In the midst of all the turbulence, the foliage plants were the calm, still center of the garden. In the corner of the garden, near the lemon tree, the delicately serrated, lime green leaves of an alpine strawberry stood out against a felty gray licorice plant, while an asterisk of aloe punctuated a drift of dark green candytuft.

Most of the perennials looked dreadful the first few months of the year, so I was grateful to the handful that held up to the rain and cold and didn't embarrass themselves by trying to flower out of season. These sturdy, modest plants were almost as useful as true foliage plants. They included my old standbys, acanthus and agapanthus, midborder plants such as Japanese anemone, as well as a few perennial groundcovers, such as snow-in-summer, candytuft, and ajuga.

Sometimes, two dormant perennials, uninteresting in themselves, made an engaging duo. That year, I noticed how lovely the columbine (*Aquilegia*) and bearded iris looked together, even out of bloom. The lacy columbine contrasted nicely with the swordlike iris. And the bluish gray-green color of their foliage matched exactly. Funny that I never had noticed before how attractive they looked together. In other seasons, the flowers must have distracted me from the leaves.

Roses

At last, I was enjoying the season. I looked around the garden and appreciated its beauty. I stopped worrying about the condition of certain slumbering plants. And I stopped feeling so anxious about my own state, too. I began to savor my specimen year.

On a sunny February morning, I pruned my roses. The job might have been tedious, but I enjoyed discovering all the little plants I had tucked into my rose borders. For instance, as I snipped and cut the 'Iceberg' florabundas by the deck, more and more orchidlike cyclamen came to light. Cutting back the roses became an adventure in excavating cyclamen. And behind the cyclamen, dark glossy fountains of naked lady (*Amaryllis belladonna*) foliage stood up handsomely. (The foliage would die down later, allowing the rose bushes plenty of space to leaf out and bloom.)

When I was finished, the border looked neat and pretty. It seemed much less stubby and bare than a border of nothing but roses would have been.

A Valentine's Day Ritual

"Don't prune the fuchsias until Valentine's Day," Paul's stepmother warned me years ago. "Otherwise, you'll stimulate new growth, which will freeze if we have another cold snap." So pruning the fuchsias became a Valentine's Day ritual. Sometimes I missed the exact date, either because bad weather kept me indoors, or because I was too busy to bother. But the year I was pregnant, I observed every ritual religiously. Valentine's Day found me in the front yard, by the living room window, positioned in front of the shrubs with my clippers in one hand and an empty bucket for the prunings at my feet.

The shrubs I faced that morning were leafless skeletons, dense with little twigs, reminders of last summer's lush growth. I cut them back hard, removing all the twigs and reducing the branches to stubs.

Paul's step-mother had explained to me that fuchsias bloom only on new growth. For that reason, they need to be pruned severely in early spring and pinched regularly during the growing season. Every nipped branch grows into two twigs and each one of those twigs grows into two more. By summer, a well-snipped fuchsia will have a dense fretwork of small branches, heavy with flowers. An ignored plant—and I have seen plenty of them in my neighborhood—will have only a few, very long branches, with scanty flowers dangling from the ends.

I cut away heaps of twigs that morning, spending fifteen minutes or so on each shrub. The slow, deliberate task gave me an opportunity to look at the planting scheme. Tall white calla lilies bloomed at the back of the border. Among the fuchsias, they seemed appropriately tropical. For the first time, however, I saw that the groundcover of sea thrift, in front, was wrong for the fuchsia border.

For one thing, the thrift was too short to be effective. The leaves hardly stood out from the Bermuda grass lawn in front of it. More importantly, though, the grassy sea thrift did not complement the tropical-looking fuchsias. The two plants simply did not belong together.

I should have realized that before. I had seen fuchsias thriving in the warmth and wet of Hawaii, and I had discovered thrift growing wild on the sea cliffs of Normandy. Nonetheless, with the arrogance of an inexperienced gardener, I had stuck incompatible plants together because I had imagined that the matching colors would look nice together. I ought to have known that creating a border isn't like accessorizing an outfit with matching shoes and belt.

When I'd finished pruning the last fuchsia bush, I threw down my clippers, took up the trowel, and dug up all the thrift. I couldn't stand to let the monstrous combination remain in the garden another day.

Out of the ground, the hunks of sea thrift looked like pieces of shaggy green carpet. Hardly any roots dangled from the plants. When I replanted them on the north side of the house, I made sure to muddy them in well so that the bottoms of the clumps made good contact with the wet earth.

Then, I looked around the garden to find a better choice for the spot beneath the fuchsias. At last, I selected dark purple *Sedum matrona* and miniature white agapanthus. I planted the border in thirds, with a mass of agapanthus between two clumps of the exotic-looking sedum. At first, when the divisions were small, the border looked worse than it had before. But soon the clumps of sedum and agapanthus spread out beneath the fuchsias.

My impetuous overhaul of the fuchsia border turned out to be a permanent improvement. The agapanthus and the sedum both grow about two feet high, tall enough to stand out clearly from the lawn. More importantly, they are both tender, lush-looking plants, suitable for a border with a tropical accent.

Iceland Poppies

One weekend in late February, I looked out the window and saw lovely saucerlike flowers blooming everywhere, dotting the borders and beds. The Iceland poppies (*Papaver nudicaule*) had roused themselves into flower while most of the garden was still asleep.

Flowers were rare and precious at that time of year, so the wealth of poppies was a wonderful luxury. The moment I glimpsed the blossoms, I ran outside across the wet grass, to pick a generous bouquet for the kitchen table. (Unlike most poppies, *Papaver nudicaule* make excellent cut flowers.) I'd planted extra seedlings, knowing that many of the flowers would end up inside the house.

Queasy among the Calla Lilies

My enjoyment of the specimen year came to a rude finish toward the end of February. Spring came to the garden and I was nauseated. The two events were not related, however. The garden did not make me sick. But I burst into sickness about the same time that the garden burst into bloom.

Though March twenty-first was still several weeks away, my California garden had hurried ahead, leaving winter behind. Suddenly, spring was manifest. My "condition," as Victorian novelists used to call it, was equally obvious. A month ago, I had thought to myself, in awe and a sort of disbelief, "Gosh I'm pregnant. I don't *feel* any different." Now, my body informed me that *everything* was different.

The Colors of Spring

Maybe I wasn't a picturesque sight, but the garden certainly was—all yellow and white and pale green. Tall white calla lilies stood at the backs of beds, while drifts of white candytuft edged the front. Self-sown white alyssum (*Lobularia maritima*) frothed everywhere, smelling sweetly of honey. White Iceland poppies bobbed on sturdy stems. Yellow lemons hung among shiny leaves. Daffodils and more Iceland poppies bloomed in similar lemony shades.

Years ago, when I planned my yellow-and-white spring garden, I took my cue from the weeds, which also bloom yellow and white in spring. I don't remember precisely which year it was when the inspiration struck me, but it was early on when the garden was new and the weeds still outnumbered the "real" flowers. I was down on my hands and knees, at eye level with the weeds. When I looked at those snow-white bells hanging on succulent stalks of onion grass and the acid-yellow flowers blooming on clumps of sour grass, I thought to myself, "Hmmm, not bad."

Yellow and white suit those days of earliest spring. The white flowers seem as fresh and cool as the March air and the yellow flowers are as cheerful as the early spring sunlight.

But the colors of early spring do not necessarily suit a later season. As the year passes, my taste changes. My affection for white blossoms lasts all year long, but my fondness for yellow flowers fades as the sun's radiance peaks.

In March, I like yellow flowers. In April, I tolerate them. In June, I dislike them. By August, I loathe them. To me, yellow seems harsh and ugly in the summer light.

For some reason, though, I don't mind seeing yellow flowers growing among vegetables. After all, tomatoes, cucumbers, pumpkins, and many other vegetables have yellow flowers, themselves. And sunflowers—the ultimate summery, yellow flower—look their best, I think, near a vegetable bed. That's why I'm glad I moved the summer-blooming yellow perennials to containers in the driveway during my big third-year plant moving frenzy.

But while I can banish yellow perennials from my back yard borders in summer, I can't always predict how the annuals will turn out. Occasionally, peach calendula or cream nasturtiums, or other annuals in my flower borders, turn out to be yellow. Or an especially vigorous Iceland poppy persists right through the year. These yellow annuals cannot stay. They must be dug out of the borders. The white poppies are welcome, but the jello-yellow ones are too bright. I like their brilliance in the silvery days of early spring. But they lose their charm under a summer sky.

Aside from a few pesky annuals, however, yellow vanishes from the back yard as spring ripens into summer. The colors grow darker and more sumptuous. Rich, coral cannas and daylilies take over. Burgundy-colored dahlias join in. Wine cups (*Callirhoe involucrata*) trail cherry red flowers over the ground. Black hollyhocks lift darkest purple flowers into the sky.

Early spring is like a lovely, intimate impressionist picture. Summer is more like a lavish baroque painting in a heavy frame.

I'm surprised how easily I managed to make the garden shift from one color scheme to another. At first, I was certain that I would never be familiar enough with the plants to orchestrate their flowering. The feat seemed impossibly complicated. So much to know! So much to plan!

I learned, however, that I can achieve almost anything in my garden as long as I don't try to accomplish too much at once. To sit down and plan a perfect garden on paper is difficult, but to arrange and rearrange a few plants every year isn't so hard. Every year, I become more familiar with the plants in my garden and more aware of my own taste. Bit by bit, I'm putting together a garden tailored to please me all year long.

Blue Flowers

That March, I noticed a few self-sown blue flowers disrupting my yellow-and-white color scheme. To my surprise, that touch of blue seemed to be just what my borders needed. The flowers looked so lovely that I let most of them stay, only yanking up the trespassers when they threatened to take over the whole yard.

A neighbor, for instance, had planted borage in her herb garden for the first time the year before, and now the plant grew everywhere in my borders. Though I pulled up dozens of borage seedlings, I also left plenty to grow. I appreciated the way the hefty plants added bulk to the bare spots in the border. The honey bees, too, liked foraging in the sky blue flowers flecked with glinting black seeds.

Forget-me-nots (*Myosotis sylvatica*) also flowered everywhere. Where they had come from I had no idea, but I suspected that they were there to stay. The fuzzy seeds clung to my socks when I worked among them, so I spread them around the garden wherever I went.

Vinca minor was another gate-crasher. I expected this one, though, for unlike the borage and forget-me-nots, I had brought the vinca into the garden myself. Years before, I planted it in the shade around the foundation of the sagging garage. Later, when the garage came down, that shady spot became the sunniest portion of the womb chamber. But the vinca survived. To my surprise, the shade-loving plant became a sun-loving plant. Even after I buried it at the bottom of a raised bed, this persistent groundcover survived, worming its way to the surface.

That spring, I let it creep over the bare ground, adding its violet-blue flowers to the array of daffodils and Iceland poppies. In April, when it finished blooming, I yanked out as much of it as I could, but I didn't worry about eradicating it completely. I knew that no matter how diligently I weeded, I would inevitably miss a few roots, and by Thanksgiving it would all be back again.

Dutch Iris

In early spring, the garden changed almost daily. Flowering bulbs faded quickly, but new ones opened to take their place. Luscious foliage sprouted in all the borders. Apple red, lime green, lemon yellow—the young leaves were as colorful as the flowers.

During those weeks, the garden evolved much faster than my pregnancy. Or so it seemed to me. As March progressed, I remained as queasy as ever, but the garden entered a whole new phase. The daffodils had faded, and the Dutch iris were beginning to bloom.

One border in the front yard looked particularly pretty that year. Near the newly emerged *Geranium* 'Johnson's Blue,' blue Dutch iris ('Ideal') and white ones ('Casablanca') floated like butterflies above a drift of forget-me-nots. A hedge of snowy candytuft contained the profusion. A touch of yellow at the throats of the iris added a bright spark, echoed by a few yellow Iceland poppies.

I particularly enjoyed the scheme, because I knew it was practical, as well as pretty. The forget-me-nots concealed a sparse-looking, semi-leafless *Salvia greggii*, while the iris foliage filled the gaps where *Gaura lindheimeri* would grow in later.

Mind the Gap

In early spring, before the perennials had grown up, I found a few holes in the borders, spots where I had forgotten to plant bulbs or poppies, and where even the rampant borage had not elbowed in. The peach border, in particular, seemed riddled with holes. The white obedient plant (*Physostegia virginiana* 'Summer Snow') had died down to the ground, while the peach lantana, 'Confetti,' had just plain died. The cannas, daylilies, and the white coneflower (*Echinacea purpurea* 'White Swan') were still little nubs.

I filled some of these gaps with winter-flowering 'Apricot' stock (*Matthiola incana*), an annual with fleecy flowers and a sweet perfume. I also lugged some of my big pots of foliage plants off the deck and into the borders. A generous clump of ferns in one spot and some big arching fans of acanthus in another brought to the patchy-looking border some welcome structure and focus.

Most of all, though, I used succulents. I placed clumps of hen-and-chicks in the bare spaces at the front of the peach border. Further back, I used jade plants. The strong, distinct forms of the jade plants stood out nicely above mounds of out-of-season perennials such as yarrow and dianthus.

To plant the succulents was nearly effortless. I broke large masses of hen-and-chicks into smaller clumps and stuck them into the ground. The clumps transplanted equally well with or without roots. The jade plants were even easier to transplant. I simply snapped branches off some of my largest specimens and poked the rootless new plants into the bald spots in the border.

I tucked succulents in everywhere, moving them around the garden like furniture or rocks. And, in fact, I moved rocks around as well. Or, actually, Paul did.

"Tell me again," Paul panted, as he crossed the lawn cradling a melon-sized dark-brown stone against his chest. "*Why* do you want this rock over here?"

"I want it to fill this bare space," I said, pointing with my toe to a gap in the peach border. "If anything fills a bare spot more easily than a succulent, it's a rock," I said.

Paul grunted. Perhaps it did not seem easy to him.

I hated to ask him to help. Ordinarily, in an unpregnant state, I never asked Paul to do any gardening. This was an exception.

"Just set it into that little hollow I dug there," I said. Rocks in the border seemed to look most natural set into the earth a bit. Left on the surface of the ground, they looked too much like a collection of dinosaur eggs.

Though Paul failed to see the beauty of rocks, to me the colors and textures were surprisingly handsome, especially on rainy days. That year, I created some interesting juxtapositions of stone and plant. A rough yellowish stone made a good neighbor to a clump of blue-toned *Festuca ovina glauca*. A round, gray, very hard-looking rock looked stunning against soft, furry lamb's ears.

Later in the season, to make room for other plants, I removed some of the succulents and Paul lugged away some of the rocks. Others, though, remained in the border all year long, among the sprawling perennials.

Time to Set Out the Seedlings

On March seventeenth, I set out my lettuce seedlings. The St. Patrick's Day planting was not a yearly ritual like the Valentine's Day fuchsia-pruning. It just happened to be a day when the seedlings were large enough to handle and the soil was dry enough to work. I planted the lettuces in a half of a wine barrel, in two concentric circles.

Over the years, the edible portion of my garden had grown modestly. I now gardened in eight half barrels, instead of five. My father-in-law, understandably proud of his own elaborate vegetable plot, was not impressed with the garden I showed him that March. By St. Patrick's Day, he already could brag about his well-caged tomato plants, his pumpkin seedlings crawling over black plastic, and his sixteen pepper plants growing snugly inside wall-o-waters. He could boast about an imposing block of corn already three inches high, and a sweep of green stubble that would soon grow into ferny carrot tops.

The barrel of lettuces may not have been as impressive as my father-in-law's twenty-foot row of green beans, but the red-and-green rosettes of the oakleaf lettuces were very beautiful.

Red and green always look beautiful together, I thought, as I admired my lettuces. I remembered my mother's holly bushes at Christmastime—red berries glowing like fiery coals among the dark green leaves—and I thought of my own winter garden, with a few jasmine leaves burning red among the green.

The colors of the lettuces were not as bright and Christmasy as the holly and the jasmine. They were more subdued and springlike—but they were intriguing all the same.

When I looked around, I found the muted reds and greens of spring elsewhere in the garden. On the rose bushes, young magenta and rust-colored foliage stood out vibrantly above the older green leaves. I'd never thought of roses as foliage plants, but now as their leaves brightened the grey misty morning for me, I realized that the shrubs were as colorful as Japanese maples.

Why do red and green always look so elegant together, so well-matched, so right? I wondered. I decided it wasn't just because they were complementary colors, but because red and green together make brown, and brown is the most natural of nature's colors.

I thought of how the artist Seurat put red dots next to blue dots, allowing the viewer's eyes to blend the colors into purple. "Maybe," I told myself, "The lettuces are really earth-brown, in their essence. Maybe nature is sometimes a pointillist painter."

Chapter Nine
One Spring Day

Mail Order Plants

When I first started gardening, my father told me, "In this life, you get what you pay for. So buy the best."

I seldom followed his advice. When I ordered plants from catalogs I was cheap and sly. First, I studied the best of the lot, flipping through their glossy pages, enjoying the lovely pictures and long, helpful descriptions. Then, I ordered from the inexpensive catalogs, with their blurry photographs and terse captions.

The year I was pregnant, I bought few plants. My landscaping projects were indefinitely postponed. Still, I couldn't bear to let the catalog season pass without buying *something*. So I ordered a groundcover, *Lamium maculatum* 'White Nancy,' some dark red columbine for the burgundy border (*Aquilegia* 'Nora Barlow') and a butterfly bush for the front yard (*Buddleia Davidii* 'Black Knight'). Not much, by some gardeners' standards. Still, I looked forward to receiving them.

One morning in mid-March, I found the small box on the front porch. It was a remarkably small box. As I carried it into the kitchen, I wondered how six plants could fit into a such a little container. When the plants were free of their wrappings and sitting on the counter, I understood how they had fit. They weren't plants at all, they were sprouts.

Though my heart sank at the sight of them, I reminded myself that after all I'd paid less than twenty dollars for the bunch. They were probably worth every penny. I tried to persuade myself that the twig in the two-inch pot *was* indeed a buddleia, and that it was just as real as the one in a five-gallon pot at the nursery. In reality, though, what I had in front of me was not a true buddleia, but only a potential buddleia.

I thought of my father's words, "You get what you pay for," and I knew he was right. But I consoled myself with a few platitudes of my own, such as, "Gardening teaches us the folly of immediate gratification. It teaches us to look toward the future. It teaches us the virtue of patience. Frugal gardeners, in that case, are the most virtuous of all."

In the end, I decided that a potential buddleia was not such a bad thing to have. After all, before I'd spent three bucks on a virtual buddleia, I'd had none at all. I couldn't have pulled one out of the air. I needed at least a twig and some roots to work with.

Feeling a bit more cheerful, I carried the plants out to the greenhouse. I knew I couldn't possibly set the snack-sized plants into a garden full of hungry snails, so I transplanted them into larger pots. Then I dosed them with fish emulsion and set them on a table to grow. With a little time and effort, I knew I could make them magnificent.

Seeds

I hadn't been inside the greenhouse for some weeks, though I'd left the door open for the cats to find shelter from the rain. In my absence, they'd made a nest in a corner out of a stack of paper bags. Some other creature—an opossum probably—had torn open a sack of blood meal.

I swept up the brown powder and put it into a tin. Then I put away the bags, set right some toppled pots, pulled some morning glory vine (!) out of a crack in the glass, and dislodged some spiders from a stack of cobwebby six-packs.

Since the plantlets had put me in a gardening mood, I decided to stay in the greenhouse and start my late-spring annuals. I already had the seeds at hand, snug and dry in an old Hershey chocolate tin.

The greenhouse was not tidy or elegant—in fact it was rather messy—but it was pleasant. As I worked, rain began to spatter down in big round drops, running down the peaked roof and along the walls. Beyond the wet glass, the garden blurred into a haze of green. It might have been a tropical rain forest or a piece of English countryside. I felt miles from home, though I was only ten feet from my kitchen door.

After I'd filled the six packs with soil, I tipped some gravel out of a pail and set off across the lawn to fetch water from the pond. The pond looked amazingly natural that morning, the lawn around it long and tousled, the rocks slick with rain. When I dipped my pail into the murky water, fish darted around my hands and a piece of submerged parrot's feather swayed like mermaid's hair at the bottom of the pond.

As I pulled out the dripping pail, I pretended to myself that the pond was a natural spring, and that fresh water would bubble out of some subterranean source to replace the gallon I had removed.

Of course, no such thing would happen. Rainwater would refill the pond. If not enough rain fell, I'd refill the pond myself with water from the hose. That morning, though, I was in the mood to indulge in fantasies. I might almost have been back in my parents' garden in the hills, pretending to be a witch or a solitary Ohlone girl. After all, what good is a garden if it's not sometimes a place of illusions?

Back in the greenhouse, I planted flowering tobacco (*Nicotiana alata*) and snapdragons—nine six packs in all. I didn't know exactly what I'd do with the flowers once they grew, but since they'd all be white flowers I didn't need to have any particular plans for them. The white accents would look lovely almost anywhere in the garden.

Saltines and Snails

The garden had outgrown its unappealing, early-in-the-season stage, but I had not. Morning sickness still troubled me. (And so did afternoon sickness and evening sickness—my nausea did not tell time.) I fought the sickness in a number of ways. Sometimes I gulped down capsules of ginger powder. I also tried pressing my thumb into the acupressure points on my wrists. Most of all, though, I ate Saltine crackers.

During those weeks, I left a trail of crumbs wherever I went—in bed, in the car, and in the greenhouse. When I planted seeds that morning, I sprinkled plenty of cracker crumbs among the seeds. "Maybe the horticulture experts will discover that Saltines are a new miracle fertilizer," I thought.

By the time I'd finished planting the seeds, the rain had stopped and the sun had come out. The garden looked green and fresh. Wet leaves sparkled in the borders.

And snails crawled everywhere.

I knew this was a perfect time to collect the snails, so I went into the house to get a plastic bag and another handful of crackers.

The task was unpleasant, but crucial. In the last two weeks, the newly hatched snails had eaten through dozens of daffodil, calla lily, and Iceland poppy buds. All around the garden, the buds were opening into flowers that looked something like paper snowflakes cut out of folded construction paper.

It was infuriating. What was worse, the snails were extremely secretive creatures. Many times during the last two weeks, I had searched for them and found only their glistening trails.

The rain, however, had enticed the tiny snails out of their hiding places. Hundreds of them dotted the spider plants, the agapanthus, the African daisies. I could gather most of them without even leaving the lawn or stepping on the wet soil in the borders.

The baby snails I plucked from the plants were lentil-sized, delicate and translucent. Two dozen of the soft-shelled creatures would have filled a teaspoon. But I didn't put them in a teaspoon, I dropped them into a plastic bag.

Bagging was the best way to deal with snails. I had experimented with other methods, but none had worked so well. Once upon a time, I thought that wood ash from the fire place was the answer. The powdery barriers certainly seemed to keep the snails away from the vulnerable plants. When the rain water washed away the ash, I could always apply more—it was free, after all. Eventually, though, I realized that the ash hardened the soil.

I also tried setting out pans of beer to trap the snails. The trick worked quite well, though it was expensive. Then early one morning I spotted a family of opossums lapping up the beer, dead snails and all. That put an end to my beer traps. Opossums are already such stupid animals, I thought, always getting themselves run over. I don't want to add to their problems by intoxicating them.

So—since I was reluctant to use poison pellets—I had to gather the snails by hand. At least, the job was quick. As I worked my way through the garden that morning, gathering snails from the wet leaves, plant after plant, I felt that the job, in a sick sort of way, was like harvesting an exotic variety of berry.

Nausea overcame me now and then as I worked, so I had to stop and frantically chew crackers for a while, until the illness subsided. The third or fourth time I stopped to munch, Paul peered over his magazine, and called down to me from the deck, "If you're feeling queasy, maybe you should find a less revolting job to do."

"I need to do *this*," I said.

Paul came down off the deck. "Slaughtering snails is not very motherly behavior," he said.

"You'd like me to stay in the greenhouse and plant seeds, eh? That's more maternal? And what do you think would happen to the seedlings six weeks from now? They'd get gobbled up as soon as I set them out. These tiny baby snails would be nickel-sized by then—and hungry."

"But all those babies," Paul said, sentimentally, staring at the plastic bag dangling from my hand.

It wasn't the babies I pitied. I saved that for the big ones that hid on the undersides of rocks, in the bulges and hollows around the swollen base of the quince tree, or in the middle of the bushy spider plants. I gathered those snails, as well, but I always felt sorry for them.

Occasionally, my fingers would brush against an unusually large, hard shell, and I would pluck loose what I imagined to be a great matriarch, with a dark brown shell the size of a walnut. I'd hold her between my thumb and finger, and study her. How had she avoided me so long? "She must be a clever one," I'd tell myself. Then, stomp! "Not clever enough," I'd say. But I respected her all the same, for knowing the good hiding places, and for surviving so long.

Weeds

After I had collected as many snails as I could find, I began to weed. The day seemed to be turning into a gardening day, although I had not planned it that way. One task led to another. Planting seeds led to collecting snails which led naturally to weeding.

As I weeded, I moved around the garden on my knees as I had moved a hundred times before. But this time, as I extracted tendrils of vinca from a large clump of daylilies, a thought struck me. I realized that my garden had moved on to a new stage. I suddenly perceived that most of the plants I was pulling out of the borders were not weeds at all—but good, honest plants that I had introduced to the garden myself, years ago.

The vinca, of course, was a holdover from a previous planting scheme. Other "weeds" were plants that I still welcomed in the borders, but which had grown too large or spread too far.

The peach border, for instance, was in danger of being colonized by spider plants. A great hulking clump had thrown out long white cords, dangling with tiny plantlets. These baby spiders had rooted wherever they touched the earth—in the ferns, in the Japanese anemone, and in a drift of crocosmia. That morning, I transplanted some of the babies to other parts of the garden. Most of them, though, went into the compost.

Who would've thought that spider plants would become pests, I thought, remembering back ten years to when I had snipped the cuttings from my mother-in-law's houseplant. Back then, the plants had seemed precious.

Where were the real weeds? For instance, where was all the sour grass? I looked around and noticed only a few clumps, frothing with yellow flowers near the fence. And what about the onion grass? Only a single sneaky white flower rose like a little flag in the center of a mounding Shasta daisy.

I shouldn't have been surprised. All through January and February, I'd weeded steadily. In fact, I'd been weeding steadily for the last ten years. I'd dug out onion grass bulbs with a trowel. And I'd kept after the sour grass diligently, excavating the long taproots. That was why I now found myself pulling perennials out of my perennial borders instead of real weeds. The balance in my garden had tipped. Now I pulled fewer weeds, but I worked harder to control the supposedly civilized plants. One struggle had replaced another.

This kind of weeding required concentration. Instead of weeding quickly, ferociously, and mindlessly, like a whirlwind or a Tasmanian devil, I needed to stop and think, to make judgements. Every time I approached a tangle of plants, I had to decide exactly how I wanted the border to look.

For example, I found some ferny salmon-colored yarrow creeping over the rhizomes of the white bearded iris. Before I could start tugging away at the yarrow or digging up the iris, I needed to decide where one drift should end and the other should begin. I had to walk away and look at the border from a distance. I had to consider the entire design.

Farther down the border, a mass of calla lilies had encircled a clump of peach-flowering daylilies. I started to dig out the callas. Then I stopped. I could see that from the calla lilies' point of view, it was the expanding clump of daylilies that needed to be restrained.

In a dozen spots around the garden I had to ask myself when a thriving plant moves beyond vigorous and becomes pesky. At what point does that nasturtium romping through a rose bush stop seeming picturesque and start looking messy? When do the ferns and Japanese anemone cease to mingle together and start to crowd each other?

All morning, I struggled with these questions. Sometimes, I solved a problem with my trowel. Ruthlessly, I dug out ferns. Afterward, the spot looked bare, and I regretted being so severe.

In other places in the garden, I decided to do nothing. I left the plants to battle among themselves. But I worried that the aggressive growers would overwhelm the more delicate plants. I fretted about a frail abutilon cowering under a canopy of acanthus leaves. Would I discover it dead next week, smothered by the larger plant?

Compared to yanking dandelions, all this judging and considering and assessing was hard. What's more, I knew this was one chore that would never end. I'd need to go on making judgements indefinitely. I might create a balance in the garden, but the equilibrium would never last long.

All the same, I wasn't crazy enough to want to go back to the previous stage, when weeds ruled my garden. I may have felt ambivalent about rampant yarrow, but I wouldn't have traded it for dandelions.

City Birds

For the rest of the morning, I dug and snipped and pulled up roving plants. I pruned a little. I sawed some firewood. Then, for a moment before lunch, I rested on the bench under the pergola.

While I was sitting there, the neighborhood parrots began to squawk in the distance, their cries a strange mixture of fury and joy. Eager to see the exotic birds, I craned my neck and was just in time to see them fly out of the palm tree on the corner, by St. Ambrose's church.

They swarmed around the palm tree like black gnats. Then they flew closer, growing larger. They swooped over rooftops, and eventually settled in the liquidambar tree next door. I could see them clearly now—small green parrots hopping about in the bare branches among the tiny hanging prickly globes.

A moment later, a sea gull flew overhead, screaming. And at the same time, a stellar blue jay in the neighbor's pine tree added its cry to the harsh music. I liked these noisy, strident bird calls. They seemed appropriate for a city garden, able to hold their own against roaring airplanes, thumping car radios, and rumbling garbage trucks.

A Gardener's Body

Inside the house, Paul was taking a pizza out of the oven. The breeze brought me the wonderful warm scent of garlic, herbs, and yeast.

I smiled out at the garden, and absently picked at a thorn in my thumb. After three months of living in a nongardener's body, my gardener's body was back.

I'd done plenty of weeding in the last couple months, but I'd never made a whole morning of it. This was the first sustained gardening I'd done all year. I examined my body, curiously—like a detective. How had I managed to make such a mess of myself in four hours?

A dozen little cuts scored my wrists. I must have got those while pulling a poof of overly aggressive snow-in-summer out of the center of a rose bush. A rash dotted my right forearm. The sap from the gazanias had done that to me—I recognized the marks. But the splinters in my thumb were a mystery. Where had those come from?

I rubbed my fingers together: the earth had sucked them dry. I looked down at my knees: they were pock-marked from the cement driveway. I touched my cheeks: they felt slightly sunburned. "Time to get organized," I thought. "The season of work has begun. Time to get out the gloves and the cushion and the sun hat, before I completely destroy myself."

I stood up. My thighs ached from squatting. My biceps throbbed from the strain of sawing up dead apricot branches for fire wood. Almost every part of my body felt different, but in a week or two, I'd be used to the aches and stings.

They say gardening is good exercise, I reflected, thinking of the newspaper stories that ran each spring. Yet those articles, with their lists of activities and charts of calories-burned-per-hour always struck as me a bit absurd. I simply didn't believe that real gardeners would do the warm-ups those articles always suggested. I just couldn't picture real gardeners doing leg stretches before pruning their roses. And I certainly couldn't imagine real gardeners getting their aerobic exercise by turning the compost.

Real gardeners turn the compost because the compost needs turning. We're not vain. When we work outside, we want to make the *garden* beautiful, not ourselves.

Good thing, too. I pitied the fool who bought a shovel and clippers hoping to garden her way to a lean and sexy body. From personal experience I could vouch that dirty fingernails and grazed knuckles are not especially provocative.

But I didn't mind. The winter me was not the real me, anyway. I wasn't comfortable with that smooth, pink and white me. That afternoon in March, as I washed my hands for lunch, I welcomed back my gardener's body.

Of Dahlias and Feminism

That day, also, Paul and I enjoyed our first alfresco meal of the year, moving our table once again out to the deck. The cats padded after us and lay at our feet, in the shade of our chairs. Raising our glasses, Paul and I toasted the spring.

When the last slice of pizza was gone, I climbed down off the deck and went over to look at the purple border. I hadn't found time to weed it, yet. I needed to cut back the morning glory vines, which snaked among the betony and tied knots around the iris. Might as well do it now, I decided.

While I was in the border tugging at the vines, I noticed the pointy-leaved dahlias emerging from the ground near the artichokes. A phrase I had read on a tee-shirt returned to me suddenly: "Women should raise more hell and fewer dahlias."

Why had the words come to me now? I must have seen that shirt years ago—probably when I was in college, when the words had no personal meaning to me, when I could no more imagine myself raising dahlias than raising a family.

Now, I was doing both. And I felt a little guilty.

I understood exactly what that tee-shirt phrase implied: "Gardening is an embarrassingly 'feminine' pursuit. It's trivial, domestic, frivolous, bland, goody-goody—and a waste of time."

With a pang, I wondered if the words could be true. I didn't think so. For me, gardening and feminism seemed perfectly compatible.

I thought back to my musings before lunch about phony gardeners, gardening their way to slimness in their elegantly casual clothes, with their expensive, ineffectual tools. That was probably why the phrase on the tee-shirt had come to me. Those frivolous gardeners deserved those words. For them, gardening was a superficial pastime, but for the rest of us? I was sure it was much, much more.

I went on working, but my lips moved silently as I argued away the doubts that the words on the tee-shirt had provoked. "In the garden, I'm free—free from crippling self-consciousness. When I garden, I never wonder, 'Does my hair look funny? Is there dirt on my face? Do these sweatpants make my bottom look big?' Instead, I appreciate the strength of my arms. I enjoy the suppleness of my back and legs. In the garden, I like my body because it *works* well.

"In the garden I'm sensuous, too—meaning that the garden arouses all of my senses. I savor the smell of the rosemary shrubs as I snip them into shape. I relish the pineapple-sweetness of a white alpine strawberry. I listen to the wind rustling through a clump of *pennisetum*. I feel the mud on my hands. And, of course, I look with hungry eyes at the beauty all around me.

"In the garden, I enjoy voluptuous experiences without thinking about myself. I *feel* myself, but I don't *think* about myself.

"This sensuousness is different from society's notion of sensuality. I grow sick, sometimes, of a sensuality always linked to appearance. In the garden, what is important is what you feel, not how you look.

"That is one kind of freedom—the freedom to forget about how my body looks and simply to enjoy the way it works. But there is another kind of freedom, too—an even better one. And that is the freedom to forget about myself altogether and lose myself in my work. Whether the work is slow and detailed, or careless and energetic, it consumes me completely. I am more interested in the work than in myself. And with that absorption comes freedom. And freedom, after all, is what feminism is about.

"So what is wrong with raising dahlias?" I finally asked myself. "If dahlias—and yarrow and iris and columbine—can free me from paralyzing self-awareness, then why not raise an acre of them?"

The Big and Small of It

Sometimes, gardening is about details, aesthetic nitpicking, about deciding whether this rose looks pretty with that fern, or whether this color is too bright or that shrub too bushy. Sometimes, gardening is about concrete, specific, even scientific questions, such as whether the soil is too sandy or too limy or not sandy enough. Sometimes, making a garden seems to be nothing more than endless fussing over details.

Then suddenly it's not about details at all. It's about the whole world.

Gardens, of course, are separate from the "real" world to a certain extent: they are fenced spaces, after all. But they're also part of the fabric of the whole world. The land that runs under those fences is connected. The gardens are all part of the same Earth. Gardens are apart and a part.

So that's why a gardener can talk one minute about a new variety of primula and the next minute about religion or environmentalism or gender politics. The pendulum can swing from the specific to the general, from the small to the large. After all, to a gardener, the word "cosmos" can signify something as small as a modest, pink flower, or as big as the entire universe.

Chapter Ten
The Middle Months

Springtime in California

Visitors from out-of-state love to say that California has no seasons. They insist that the months from February to April are one long dragged-out semispring; a pseudospring of rain and darkness and sun and flowers and more rain and then more flowers. One step forward and one step backward, never really going anyplace.

It's true that spring in California comes gradually— shyly, almost. Our first taste of spring has nothing to do with the calendar. The calendar says it is February, but the daffodils, Dutch iris, and trees are already in full bloom, along with such cool-weather annuals as pansies, stock and Iceland poppies.

Then, after a glorious beginning, there is a lull, almost a second winter, usually toward the end of March. In the garden, then, there are as many signs of death as of new life. The bulbs and winter annuals fade. The daffodil and Dutch iris leaves grow floppy and yellow. The flowers on the poppies become smaller. The foliage starts to yellow. The sweet-smelling stock goes into the compost. Adding to the melancholy atmosphere, the end of the month usually brings dark, wet days.

In April, the weather improves. At last, the sun burns brightly and the perennials perk up. By May, the garden is bursting with bloom once again.

This sequence of events is not unlike spring in other parts of the country. Most gardeners enjoy bulbs first, perennials later. The difference is that the whole affair is drawn out in California. Our first paperwhite narcissi often bloom around Halloween, although October—with its falling leaves and jack o'lanterns—hardly seems springlike. In a sense October is a beginning in California, as well as a winding down, for though the calendar year is drawing to an end, the rainy season has just begun. It can last through May, and sometimes go into June. Not surprisingly, then, October to June and is the real growing season for flowers in California. Most bulbs and perennials bloom during these fertile months. After June, California gardens grow dry and dusty. Only the most drought-resistant perennials and grasses thrive in summer and into autumn, bringing a different, more severe, kind of beauty to our gardens.

In the wet, warm, luscious days of late spring, however, our gardens are as green and opulent as springtime gardens anywhere.

Plump April

During the year I was pregnant, the small developments —the unfurling leaves, the buds ballooning into spheres— interested me as much as the spectacular bursts of bloom. I especially appreciated the period in mid-April when the perennials were all plumping up and preparing to flower. Naturally, I looked forward to the gorgeous blossoms that would come later, but I also enjoyed the stage before the blossoms.

During those April days, the perennials seemed to grow more ample and healthy by the hour. Around the womb chamber, the clumps of *Geranium*, 'Wargave Pink,' swelled up. They didn't put out runners; their bases didn't expand. All the same, the plants grew larger. They seemed to inflate.

The snow-in-summer under the 'Iceberg' roses puffed up too, growing lush and thick. Already, a few buds spangled its wooly foliage. Thousands of winter-white flowers would soon transform the gray groundcover into a spectacular carpet of "snow," but I couldn't help thinking that the plant was at its most attractive now. That full, rounded, just-on-the-cusp stage was extremely appealing.

Perhaps I paid more attention to the subtle changes in the garden that year because I was also paying attention to every small change in myself. By April, I was also starting to grow. My middle was beginning to thicken. I had to wear my shirts untucked. When I bent down to deadhead a pansy, or when I stretched up to thin the fruit on the nectarine trees, the ligaments in my abdomen twinged sharply, confirming that the organization of things inside me was changing bit by bit.

Crazy for Corms

In April, the kids down the block began to play ball in the street again. The guy in the house behind ours practiced his oboe on his back porch once more. Paul and I were able to picnic on the lawn. And the freesias and sparaxis were there to welcome us.

These corms were so robust, so bright and jolly, that they put to shame the fragile bulbs that had come before. In retrospect, the bulbs seemed insipid. "Stupid bulbs," I thought, "Why do I pay so much money for you and go to the trouble of chilling you in the fridge and planting you out every year, when I could buy inexpensive corms instead and enjoy them forever?"

In the womb chamber, behind some candytuft, cream-colored freesias bloomed among yellow Iceland poppies. The yellow poppies brought out the golden bee-lines in the freesias' throats. At the same time, dozens of maroon sparaxis bloomed in the burgundy border, behind the grey lamb's ears and 'Mahogany' nasturtiums, which twisted and coiled and mounded over the sparaxis' bladelike foliage.

Near those maroon sparaxis, the last of the tulips bloomed in pots. This juxtaposition underscored the difference between the formal, solemn bulbs and the easygoing, unpretentious corms. Those pale apricot and ice-white tulips were lovely, but they were guests in my garden— elegant and polite, but not at ease. They were somber and decorous, like dignified foreigners. In contrast, the sparaxis lived up to their name, the "harlequin flower." They were cheerful, unrefined, and very much at home.

Coralbells

In April, the coralbells (*Heuchera sanguinea*) also prepared to bloom. The pink stems with buds like miniature asparagus spears telescoped upward, looking, at first, awkward and rather funny edging a border in the front yard. For a while, I wondered if I had been wrong to put them at the front of the border. They neither billowed like lobelia nor crept like ajuga. In fact, they didn't seem to grow much at all. Instead of expanding outward, the coralbells had a peculiar way of pushing themselves, roots and all, out of the earth, forcing me to dig up a few of the particularly elevated ones and set them firmly in the ground again.

"What a nuisance!" I thought.

Then, in late April, the pink flowers opened, and they looked so nice that I forget all my complaints.

The white version, 'June Bride,' pleased me less. The white looked dull and didn't gleam. Moreover, in certain light, the delicate wands were invisible.

An Odd Couple

The spring garden was full of surprises and satisfactions —as well as small disappointments. So much happened all at once. The plants linked themselves in different alliances —annuals with foliage plants, bulbs among succulents, or perennials against shrubs.

One of my favorite plant marriages that year was silly rather than beautiful. In the front yard, I'd planted several round, neatly clipped rosemaries (*Rosmarinus officinalis*) to give structure to a border filled with hillocks of *Geranium* 'Johnson's Blue,' and other soft, mounding plants. Of course, when I planted the rosemaries I hadn't known that forget-me-nots would seed themselves all over the border.

In April, when most of the perennials were still in bud, the rosemaries bloomed among the self-sown forget-me-nots, their blue-flecked balls sitting stolidly in the romping, unruly mass of blue. The similarity of the flowers accentuated the difference in their shapes. The two plants looked wonderfully goofy together.

Prima Donnas and Supporting Players

When the row of 'Iceberg' florabundas by the deck exploded into bloom, trumpets should have sung out. Those shrubs were aggressively gorgeous.

Because of their prominent position in the garden, we couldn't escape their beauty. At breakfast, when Paul and I sat on the deck, their, heavy, nodding clusters of white flowers rose above the planters of succulents. At noon, when we ate picnic-style on the lawn, the blooms blared out at us from behind the other low-growing flowers.

Hadn't I read somewhere that white flowers are supposed to be calm, peaceful, and accommodating? Hadn't I heard that they are useful for easing transitions between other, bolder colors? The books were wrong. I couldn't imagine flowers more brazen than those white roses. Scarlet palargoniums and orange dahlias could not have flashed more flashily.

Other comparatively sedate supporting players bloomed around the roses' ankles. Usually, the roses stole my attention away from them. Sometimes, however, when I sat on the lawn reading a book or magazine, my eyes strayed toward that part of the garden. Then, I appreciated the groundcovers and little flowers that blossomed at eye level.

A blanket of gray snow-in-summer covered the front of the border, spangled with tiny white flowers echoing the white roses above. Clumps of sea thrift broke up the smooth mantel of groundcover and matched the fuchsia-colored ixia that bloomed among the roses, shooting up a yard high on fantastically wiry stems. Compared to the big, lush roses, these little flowers were insignificant. Yet they enriched the border, without muddling it or distracting from the main feature.

Perspective

During those long afternoons on the lawn, I saw the garden from a new angle, a perspective close to a cat's. I noticed distressing minutiae, such as the fact that the bindweed was creeping from the roses into the lawn. But I noticed beautiful details, as well—the velvety texture of an indigo pansy, and the pale peach splotches in the throat of a creamy nasturtium.

Often I lay on my side (being unable to lie on my stomach, any more) and watched long-legged waterskeeters dance over the pond. Below them, goldfish flickered in the murky water, and above them, the everpresent dragonflies hovered and darted. At those moments, the pond seemed to be a tiny, perfect world.

When I dressed in the mornings, I saw the garden from a different perspective. I saw it from a distance. Framed by the open window, the pond glinting in the sunlight was dramatic—solid and brassy, like a shield.

It's the same pond, I thought, remembering the waterskeeters and the goldfish, the wet rocks and the cool, damp, intimate smell. Yet it was a very different pond, too. Instead of a home for various insects, a perfect microcosm, a complex little place, it seemed more like a part of the whole garden, a design detail, a "garden feature."

Everything else also seemed different from that distance. The nasturtiums I knew so well were a blur of creamy yellow on the fence, while the black pansies were completely invisible.

Instead, I could see the world beyond my garden. The porch where my neighbor, the oboe-player, liked to practice loomed above the back fence. Slices of other yards showed, too—a piece of someone's garage, some distant pine trees, a chimney, a towering acacia. My garden was only a little piece of what I saw from my window, so the space seemed small. But when I lounged on the lawn, with my eyes skimming across grass, the garden seemed immense. The close view and long view were both true views, I realized.

Hot Hot Hot

Myosotis, Alyssum, Heuchera sanguinea, Dianthus barbatus are Valentine flowers—dainty plants, lacy bits of froth. Their popular names sound like old-fashioned poetry: "Forget-me-nots, basket of gold, coralbells, sweet William."

By May Day, these early flowers began to fade. By Mother's Day most of them were gone. The carnival that suddenly broke out in June swallowed up any lingerers. In the front yard, the last of the coralbells looked feeble beside such big-elbowed plants as daylilies. Next to tall, bright bearded iris, the forget-me-nots paled—and soon began to mildew sadly.

The flowers that replaced them were big. Easter lilies shaped like megaphones. Dahlias as large as saucers, if not dinner plates. Tall, chunky snapdragons. Crowds of iris. Tumbling, disorderly masses of yarrow.

And bright. Every gaudy shade of movie star lipstick gleamed in the late-spring borders. 'Gloria' palargonium: orange-red. 'Black Pearl' dahlia: deep raspberry. Wine cups: cherry pink.

In June, Technicolor ruled the garden, and I loved it. I could barely remember the pale yellows and creams and fragile blues of February. Since then, the light had deepened, the air had warmed, the colors and smells had intensified.

As the world outside had gone on, I had galloped along with it, and I didn't want to look back. In June, if someone had handed me a bouquet of March daffodils, I would have snarled ungratefully. Lilies intoxicated me, now. I'd gone on, past daffodils. I couldn't see the *point* of daffodils. They were like the thin, watery sun of early spring. To hell with pastels. I wanted color the way a hungry lion wants blood.

Fed Up with Foliage

When I first started gardening, pale pink and lavender were the colors I saw most often in the professional gardens photographed for books and magazines. People in the know seemed to prefer pale blossoms. To them, a scarlet canna lily was the equivalent of a loud belch.

Later, after I had been gardening for a few years, I realized that the trend had changed. Ultrarefined gardeners were giving up flowers entirely. Now, they lived for foliage. Everyone, from professional landscapers to amateur gardeners, favored leaves.

Garden writers expressed the trend succinctly: "Plant for foliage," they wrote. "And think of flowers as an added bonus." Garden photographers glorified the trend with close-up shots of sweet woodruff leaves grazing ajuga foliage, or graceful blades of ornamental grasses brushing up against jadelike sedum.

To a certain extent, I admired foliage. I recognized that evergreen plants such as ferns, box shrubs, and sturdy rosemaries both sustained the winter landscape and carried the garden through the midsummer blahs. In February, I had adored my aloe and Mediterranean fan palms and acanthus leaves. In August I would swoon over my purple fountain grass. But in June, this fashionable infatuation with leaves seemed almost perverse.

It was the peak of the year. The days were long. A blood-colored sun lingered till nine and returned just a few hours later for a silvery dawn. The year seemed to swing up to a peak and stay suspended there. At that moment of vivid, keen stillness, I wanted all around me vibrant flowers that echoed the intensity I felt in the sky and the sun.

I was skeptical of this passion for foliage plants, because I knew it was a learned love. I only had to consider my own experience to know that flowers naturally come first. As a child, I hadn't thought of admiring a plant because it was nubby gray or glossy green, or because it offered arching stems, or leaves etched with gold. But I adored honeysuckle at the age of two. I was born loving flowers; I had to learn to like leaves.

I also knew it was an acquired taste because Paul didn't share it. When I, an educated and enlightened gardener, exclaimed over a graceful clump of *Miscanthus sinensis*, Paul called me a snob. He was right, in a way. It *was* snobby to prefer foliage plants in tasteful greens and grays and occasionally muted golds or burgundies, to the shock of bubble-gum pink roses. Luckily, I'd never been enough of a snob to banish flowers from my garden, as some gardeners had.

Styles change, of course. These days, more and more gardeners seem willing to experiment with colorful flowers. That June, though, when foliage was so fashionable, I felt more forcefully than ever before the power of brilliant color. Diehard foliage gardeners must be not just snobby, but also timid, it seemed to me. They must be afraid of seeming vulgar, and maybe also afraid of being touched by the force of vivid color.

Color did not scare me at all. Or if it did, then perhaps I enjoyed being scared a little.

All the same, the flowers in my late spring garden were incredibly demanding. That was their drawback. That June, as I wandered through the garden admiring the flowers, holding a fistful of dahlias, snuffing all the scent out of a trumpet lily, gazing ardently at a tangle of blue bachelor's buttons and orange California poppies, I noticed that the lily, though lovely, was already beginning to fade, the bachelor's buttons needed deadheading, and the dahlias were slightly mildewed.

The foliage plants were easier, without a doubt. The fan palm and the *Asparagus meyeri* just stood in my garden all year, looking striking. Maybe that was why so many people seemed to prefer their kind of easy good looks.

How simple gardening would be if I grew nothing but foliage plants. I wouldn't need to orchestrate blooming time.

I also would avoid shocks and disappointments, such as discovering that 'Apricot Bon-Bon' calendula is bright orange and not apricot at all. I would have time to relax and enjoy the garden, instead of running around with clippers, deadheading constantly. Most importantly, I would have a peaceful, quiet garden. My summer garden was decidedly *not* quiet.

As spring passed into summer, that year, and the flowers in my garden became more brazen day by day, I was glad I wasn't a foliage gardener. The flowers were worth the work. I wanted to shake those pallid leaf-lovers by their narrow shoulders and say, "Mix some flowers into all that foliage, and one morning in June you'll go wild with joy because the world is so varied and so beautiful."

Delirious

I could remember, though, one year when I had overdone the color. It was the fourth year, the year of the shirley poppies.

If I hadn't found myself with a nice large empty flower bed, the scheme would never have come into being. But the lovely bare dirt around the womb chamber tempted me. "Thank goodness all those perky yellow and white flowers are gone," I thought. "Now, I can create something more complex and alluring." So I sketched out a rough plan, spread compost, planted seeds and seedlings and some dahlia tubers. Then I went off to France and Switzerland with Paul for five weeks.

We returned from our vacation one night in June. The journey from the door of the hotel in Geneva to our own front door had taken twenty-four hours, so I was too dazed to look at the garden when I arrived home. I dragged myself past the ghostly 'Lady Banks' roses blooming over the porch and tottered into the house, thinking vaguely that the place seemed smaller than I remembered, wondering if the garden would seem shabby, too.

The next morning, I woke up early and went straight outside. A hot sun was rising over the hills. I glanced around the garden and was stunned . . . the bed encircling the womb chamber had grown into something surreal.

A hedge of coral-pink dahlias encircled the patio of broken concrete in the center of the womb chamber. Skirting the dahlias, fibrous-rooted begonias of the same bright coral had grown a foot tall and were completely spherical, like pink hedgehogs. Crowds of shirley poppies—mostly red, but with a few mottled pinks here and there—stood behind the dahlias.

A lone coreopsis, which had escaped my assault on yellow plants, bloomed bountifully next to the single exclamation point of a delphinium. I have no idea why the delphinium was there. I had decided years before that delphiniums were too temperamental for my garden. Yet, there it was, deep sapphire, between the sunny, daisy-flowered coreopsis and the red poppies.

The dazzling, color-saturated flowers seemed to conspire, encouraging each other to dazzle more brightly. The dahlias looked much pinker next to the coreopsis than they'd appeared in the plant catalog. And the poppies next to the delphinium looked redder than anything I'd ever seen before.

Not a single foliage plant or white flower offered a break in the bright circle. There was no breathing space at all, just spicy color.

That first morning, I wandered into the ring of flowers and sank onto the patio bench. As the sun beat down on my head, a bumblebee tumbled in a coreopsis flower and an orange monarch butterfly ate from a red poppy, clashing gorgeously. For several minutes I was too dazed to move. I felt like Alice in Wonderland, or Dorothy among the poppies.

Perhaps in the normal foggy weather of a Bay Area summer, Paul and I would have welcomed such brilliance in our garden. That summer, however, turned out to be unusually hot. The colors danced and vibrated wherever we looked. To glance out the window was to be suddenly assaulted by a tempest of color.

The color reminded me of clothes my father had worn in the early seventies. I kept waiting for Lucy in the Sky with Diamonds to float by and smile down on my garden. I expected potheads to wander through saying, "Wow, man . . .," in dazed wonderment. As it was, my guests, even without benefit of mind-numbing drugs, were almost rendered speechless, able only to say, "My god."

I felt perpetually jet-lagged that summer—groggy—as though I never had recovered from my vacation. The cats suffered, too. All summer they skulked around the yard looking put upon.

To my surprise, the water bill for the month Paul and I had been away turned out to be twice the normal amount. My father had watered the garden for us while we were on vacation. He had been diligent about it. Very diligent, he said. But after all, I pointed out, all those unwashed dishes and untaken showers ought to have kept the water consumption down.

Finally, my father confessed that he accidentally had left the hose on overnight and had returned the next day to find the womb chamber—the lowest part of the garden—under four inches of water.

That explained it. That extra-deep watering, on top of all the compost I had added before our trip and my own bizarre planting scheme, had resulted in a garden on acid.

Bountiful Blossoms

That fourth summer I learned that flowers alone do not make a garden. Nevertheless, I always have had an appetite for big flowers. My hunger for them has never cooled. Something about a big flower on a strong stem satisfies my soul. I like flowers I can hold in my fist and stick my nose into— flowers that look like the flowers in a child's drawing.

Running through the seasons, these flowers include calla lilies, daffodils and tulips, Iceland poppies, Transvaal daisies, roses, lilies, oriental poppies, sunflowers, and dahlias.

They do not include those little blossoms that grow on shrubs like popcorn. No *Salvia greggii*, no *Gaura lindheimeri*, no lavender, no perennial wallflower (*Erysimum* 'Bowles Mauve.') None of those drought-resistent woody plants that gradually have become the backbone of my garden.

The year I was pregnant, I took no notice at all as those dependable shrubby plants began to bloom, adding their bits of confetti color to the landscape. But I noticed the oriental poppies (*Papaver Orientale* 'Princess Victoria Louise') preparing to bloom in the womb chamber. I saw the long, sprawling, jagged leaves start to upright themselves. The plants had been like hands all spring, lying flat, palms up. Now, in June, the fingers began to close, and out of the closed fingers rose thick, hairy stalks.

Soon the ends of the stalks began to swell into huge apricot-shaped buds. I watched them every day, and grew excited on the evening when I glimpsed a bit of pink showing through a crack in the largest bud. The next morning, I discovered that a great crinkly-petaled poppy had opened in the night.

The poppy was seven inches across, shrimp pink, with black blotches around the center, and it floated on a four-foot stem. "Now *that's* a flower," I told myself.

At the same time, the 'Black Dragon' lilies (*Lilium leucanthum centifolium*) began to bloom among the 'Iceberg' roses along the edge of the deck, saturating the air with their decadent scent.

As the summer progressed, the flowers in my garden seemed determined to outdazzle each other. In May, the roses had struck me as outrageously gorgeous flowers, but now in June, they were only conventionally pretty, like little girls in party dresses. Beside them, the lilies were grown-up beauties. With their streaky purple trumpets and creamy interiors, the lilies looked exotic and slightly ugly, in the way that very beautiful people sometimes look ugly.

One afternoon, when Paul and I were eating lunch on the deck, he complained to me, "Your lilies are staring at us."

He was right, the lilies did seem to turn haughty faces toward us. But I loved them for their insolence. June seemed to be the month for arrogance in the flower borders—for color-drenched dahlias, exotic oriental poppies, and lilies of almost eerie beauty.

Enjoying It All

In June that year, when the borders were at their most dazzling, an old high-school friend visited—with her six-month old baby in tow. "Enjoy all this while you can," she urged me. "Wait until next year, when you have a baby. You won't have time to *look* at your garden, much less to work in it." And gesturing out at the borders she said, "All this will be solid weeds."

So I watched the garden closely. I paid attention to the bright rich flowers in my summer garden, just as I had paid attention to mud and foliage in my winter garden, and to the fragile beauty of the blossoms of early spring. Every development seemed miraculous.

The Quickening

I also felt my baby move for the first time that June. For weeks, I'd been waiting for the moment and wondering what it would be like. My friend described the feeling as a kind of flutter, so whenever a monarch butterfly or a yellow swallowtail tumbled through the sky, I thought to myself, "It will feel like that."

But it didn't, quite—although it was a wonderful feeling. It was more like the wiggle of a worm, wriggling deep in the dark.

The baby wriggled and I put my hand on my belly and thought, "Hello, little worm."

Making Pictures

My sister-in-law offered to throw a baby shower for me, but Paul and I decided to host the party ourselves. We wanted to skip the silly games—the cake shaped like a diaper-pin, and the pink-and-blue centerpieces—and have a simple garden party instead, with friends and family relaxing on the lawn, celebrating summer as well as our baby.

Before the party, I spent a frenzied day getting the garden ready. I perked up the peach border with a few groups of 'Peaches 'n' Cream' verbena, which looked lovely in front of the salmon yarrow, the coral *salvia greggii* and the 'Apricot Glow' abutilon. I also added some snapdragons to the bare spaces in the other borders.

I did not, however, want to spend a lot of money on annuals, so instead of buying flats and flats of new plants, I improved the borders by cutting away the plants that were already there.

By late June, the garden certainly needed cutting back. It was starting to look sloppy. In the front yard, the Shasta daisies had grown a yard high, the weight of their buds pulling them forward onto the grass. The Russian sage (*Perovskia*) had grown tall and wispy, too. I cut the leggy plants back hard, postponing their flowering for a few more weeks in exchange for shorter, sturdier plants in the long run.

Pruning not only improved the plants themselves, it also helped to tidy the beds. Best of all, the cutting back revealed "lost" plants. All day, I found myself excavating old friends I'd forgotten.

For instance, when I cut back the Shasta daisies, I incidentally revealed some sweet William that had been completely engulfed. When I snipped the Russian sage, I gave the lamb's ears some breathing space. Each time I cut away something, I felt as though I were creating a new picture.

The climax of the morning came when I pulled out some calla lilies by the living room window in the front yard and discovered a neglected fuchsia at the back of a border, where it had been struggling to grow in almost total darkness. I wondered what to do with that buried treasure, whether to move it to a better spot or leave it where it was.

In the end, I decided to dig up the front portion of the calla lilies, leaving a semicircle of them behind the fuchsia. That way, the plant would receive enough light to flower, and its cotton-candy pink blossoms would stand out strikingly in a cave of dark green foliage.

While I cleared out the borders, my family helped prepare for the party in other ways. My mother brought over benches and pots of flowers from her own garden. Paul mowed the lawn and washed the grime and cobwebs off the greenhouse.

When we had finished, the garden was impeccable, with an edged lawn and groomed borders. I couldn't remember it ever before looking so polished. With my family's help, I had achieved the all-but-impossible—a tidy, weed-free garden.

I stopped and glanced around the yard, trying to memorize the moment. Too much of the time, the future preoccupied me. I was forever looking forward to next month when this flower would bloom or to next year when that fruit tree would begin to bear. I remembered what my friend had said, "Wait until next year, when you have a baby!" I had no idea what my garden would look like next summer, so I concentrated on appreciating it now.

The Stork Party

Most of the chatter at the party was about babies, but some of the guests talked to me about my garden too. Like any gardener, I enjoyed their praise. To be honest, I preferred to be congratulated on my roses more than I did on my pregnancy, for so far I had taken more trouble over the roses. Baby-making, up to that point, seemed fairly effortless.

Gardening, however, certainly was not effortless. That was obvious. Still, I didn't know how much credit to take. Very little of the garden had been worked out on graph paper. Most of its loveliness was a result of fiddling around. Weather and accidental deaths and births had influenced it, too.

The afternoon of the stork party, I realized that the story of the garden was rather like my own story: a mixed-up tale of schemes and accidents, of hard work and good luck. From one point of view, Paul and I seemed to be extremely calculating people. We had planned our baby, choosing exactly when to have it. We were saving money carefully, so that we'd be able take time off to be with the baby when it came. Everything we had done—from buying our house while we were still in college to planning our family—was thought out carefully ahead of time and discussed endlessly.

And yet, sometimes in spite of all our planning my life astonished me. That afternoon, the baby kicked me. A hummingbird hovered nearby, drinking from a honeysuckle vine. I felt life pulse all around me and inside of me. This *was* life and I was astonished.

How did this happen? How did I get here? When did I set out on this path?

Dusk came. The pergola sent strong shadows across the lawn in a checkerboard of light and dark. My friends and family gathered on the deck. I was proud to have a place to invite them to. I was flattered that people from all over the Bay Area had come together in my garden.

A family friend proposed a toast. We raised our champagne glasses. Mine was full of something that looked suspiciously like apple juice, but never mind. The moment was exquisite. We drank in silence for a second. Dragonflies darted and hovered over the pond. Inside me, the baby leapt.

How much of my life had I shaped? How much was unplanned? I couldn't answer those questions. Then I looked at the garden—that complex, living space, created part by chance and part by design—and I knew that the answer did not matter.

Plums and Nectarines

Certainly the espaliered fruit trees were not shaped by chance. Every winter, I pruned them carefully, repeating the cuts illustrated in a gardening book.

That summer, the trees finally looked good enough to justify the effort of caring for them. The branches and trunks were thick and strong; the crop was heavy. Volunteer fennel plants (seeded by a bird?) grew in the womb chamber near some yarrow, and the frothy, lacy plants had attracted beneficial insects. As a result, the fruit on the fruit trees was almost without blemish.

Unfortunately, the lady bugs and parasitic wasps could do nothing about snails. "Who ever heard of snails attacking fruit trees?" Paul asked.

I shrugged. None of the books I'd read mentioned the problem. Probably mollusks don't often bother to climb the trunks of ordinary trees, but they glided right up our wooden fence and feasted on the ripe fruit.

Fortunately, they left some for us. That summer, Paul and I feasted, too. The fence both reflected heat and sheltered the trees, so that their fruit ripened quickly and tasted sweet. Paul and I sat on the lawn and ate warm plums and nectarines just three feet away from the trees where the fruit had grown.

The trees looked very summery, with their bright fruit and light green foliage. The purple plums and red-gold nectarines stood out beautifully against the gray, weathered redwood fence. The long, drooping leaves grew thickly, making the branches shaggy and lush.

I remembered the pink blossoms of February on the leafless branches and I thought of myself back then, thin but nauseated and depressed, wondering if my condition would go on for the rest of my life. Now, I was getting big and the baby was getting big. Time had passed, after all.

I liked to think that the summer garden was feeding the baby. I liked to feel that some of the richness in the garden was reaching the small creature inside me, and that the baby was gorging on all that vitality, just as I was gorging on plums. I liked to think that the baby was getting fat on summer.

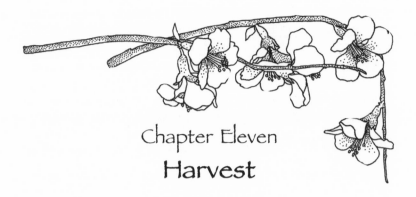

Chapter Eleven
Harvest

Fog and Sun

In July, the usual summer fog settled in. It wasn't the creeping, misty fog of a romantic film, but a high white glaring fog. It made the garden dull. No shadows played about the borders. No sunlight sparkled on the dewy grass. Time seemed frozen. Nine in the morning looked like noon and noon looked like four in the afternoon.

During that foggy month, the temperature rarely rose above sixty. When Paul and I sat outside, we wore sweats instead of shorts. The green tomatoes on the vines in the half-barrels stayed green indefinitely, and the bell peppers stopped setting bud.

Soon, the plants became as ashen-colored as the sky. Mildew spread across the dahlia leaves, crept up the Lady Banks roses on the front porch, and stained the vines of the lemon cucumber. Rust peppered the underside of the snapdragons' slender leaves.

With August, the weather changed again. At last we had a real summer, the kind that people in other parts of the country take for granted. The fog vanished. The sun shone. The mildew on the dahlias and roses cleared up. And one fine day, the lettuces bolted. That was the sign I'd been looking for. When I discovered those tapering green spires (like some exotic kind of religious architecture), I knew the hot weather had arrived at last.

Paul and I were grateful for the sun, for we needed it almost as much as the tomatoes and cucumbers did. We longed to feel it soak into our fog-soggy bones. With the heat, though, the garden lost some of its early summer sensuality. It became dry, bleached out, and drowsy. The lawn took on a brownish cast. The hen-and-chicks lost their plumpness and shriveled slightly, until they resembled bunches of dried roses dyed a curious gray-blue.

The season of big flowers ended. The lilies, agapanthus, oriental poppies, and daylilies all finished for the year.

The few big flowers that did bloom in August seemed eccentric. The naked ladies (*Amaryllis belladonna*), for instance, looked bizarre rather than beautiful. In the border by the deck, the leafless stems snaked upward through the dense rose foliage and raised big pink trumpets toward the sky. The color of the flowers appeared wrong for the plants. They should have bloomed in a sophisticated burgundy or decadent mauve, rather than that naive cotton-candy pink.

The dahlias—which continued to produce batches of hefty, jewel-toned flowers—also looked slightly odd in August. They seemed different now that they no longer mingled with other opulent blossoms. They were precious, like the first daffodils in February. But like those first daffodils, they seemed out of character with the rest of the garden. They even seemed slightly unsuitable.

Informal plants were a better match for the garden's more relaxed, uncomplicated mood. The ornamental grasses were in bloom and they suited the dry summery garden far better than the dahlias did. I often found myself admiring a clump of grass backlit by the morning sun or swaying in the late afternoon breeze.

The purple fountain grass (*Pennisetum setaceum* 'Rubrum') in the burgundy border along the back fence was seven years old and had, over time, grown into a tall, dramatic plant. It was especially striking in bloom, with glossy red-black plumes arching down like a swan's neck over the gray-leaved licorice plants and lambs ears.

Its green-and-pink cousin, *Pennisetum orientale*, was a less stately plant, but a much friendlier one. From a distance, the three clumps in the bed around the womb chamber looked like a family of porcupines out for a walk. The furry pinkish-tan plumes stood up tall above the round hillocks of grass green foliage.

Other perennials with buff-pink flowers bloomed in the near the clumps of fountain grass. *Sedum spectabile* 'Brilliant' was my favorite of these plants. While it also blended well with purple flowers, such as *Liatris spicata* 'Kobold,' and betony (*Stachys officinalis*) in the purple border, it seemed equally at home with pink blossoms in the womb chamber planting.

Its form was wonderfully distinct. The flat flowerheads contrasted well with the vertical grass plumes, while the succulent, almost crunchy, foliage looked interesting against the narrow, sharp blades of grass.

Next to the sedum, yarrow bloomed with broad, flat flowerheads much smaller than the sedum's, but similarly shaped and similarly colored. The yarrow's flowers opened purplish pink and faded in time to brownish pink. And because yarrow flowered for such a long time, the colors from each stage of bloom were present on the plant simultaneously.

Between the grass and the yarrow, jewel-toned, 'Black Pearl,' dahlias bloomed in a vibrant raspberry red. Since the dahlia's leaves were much less interesting than the blades of grass, the ferny yarrow foliage, or the succulent sedum stalks, I had tucked the dahlias into a concealed spot, hiding the leaves. As a result, the flowers seemed to float among the pale greens and dusty pinks of the other plants— blotches of pure color. The plumes of fountain grass looked especially rosy against those pink dahlias.

The whole arrangement was serene, summery, and un-ashamedly arid-looking. I even added a long piece of drift-wood and a few smooth rocks to emphasize a dry, bleached seaside look.

The cats often visited the bed around the womb cham-ber. During those hot August days, they hid like lions in the shadows beneath the grasses. In the cooler evenings, they sharpened their claws on the driftwood, chased imaginary creatures through the swishing grass, and draped them-selves over the sun-warmed rocks for their after-dinner naps.

Those clumps of grass made all the difference in the late-summer garden. They gave August its own distinct look and prevented it from becoming simply a paler, drier version of July.

Down on the Farm

One day toward the end of August, when Paul and I were sitting on the bench in the womb chamber, near the swaying grasses, Paul suddenly said that he knew why ornamental grasses complemented the summer garden so perfectly.

"It's because they suggest fields of wheat or the wide-open prairies. They're like chunks of Kansas dropped down into the garden."

This struck me as quite appropriate; after all, summer is the quintessentially American season.

All during that long rainy winter and through the lush warm spring, tantalizing pictures of English flower gar-dens had floated through my imagination as I worked in my garden. But in August, when the weather grew hot, dry, and decidedly un-English, the flowers faded, and the veg-etables began to flourish, I forgot about Sissinghurst and Great Dixter and become a patriot. During that month, I actually pitied English gardeners for not being Americans. I stopped trying to be Vita Sackville-West presiding over magnificent borders, and instead pretended to be that ultra-American character: a farmer.

Tomatoes

Tomatoes were the mainstay of my vegetable garden. I couldn't imagine an easier way to satisfy the dream of being a farmer-for-a-month than by tending a couple of rugged tomato plants.

Over the years, I had tried many different tomato varieties. In my third or fourth year of gardening, I did the heirloom thing, growing several highly acclaimed varieties of old-fashioned tomatoes, and pinning most of my hopes on a variety called 'Brandywine.' So many testimonials in magazines and books had described its superior flavor that I expected it to be sensational.

From April through July, I tended the Brandywine vine conscientiously and it grew well. I became so eager to taste the fruit that my mouth watered whenever I passed the plant. Then in August, my prize plant yielded exactly three tomatoes and died. The tomatoes tasted okay, I think, but to be honest, I can hardly remember what they tasted like at all.

The year I was pregnant, I decided to be lazy. I wasn't in the mood to fuss over feeble vines, so I stuck with the vigorous, productive hybrids I'd grown in the past. I planted two Early Girls, one Sweet One Hundred, and one yellow-fruited Lemon Boy. I harvested a bumper crop.

The Early Girls alone flooded us with small, sweet, blood-red fruits. Paul and I ate them at nearly every meal, and we still had plenty left over. The kitchen was always full of racks of drying tomatoes.

I vowed then not to waste another season on heirloom varieties. "Why should I?" I asked myself, "When hybrids are such stalwart plants." And more than that, I found something very comforting, very American about hybrid tomatoes with names such as Early Girl, Big Boy, Better Boy, and Beefsteak. The companies that sold the seeds seemed very American, too. That year, I'd bought my packets of seeds from a catalog illustrated with photographs of sunburned kids standing next to massive jack o'lantern pumpkins, and munching on ears of sweet white corn—and, of course, demonstrating that one slice of beefsteak tomato covered their entire hamburger.

"My grandfather grew beefsteak tomatoes," I told myself. "He wouldn't have wasted his time on sickly non-hybrids, either."

Vegetables Feed My Fantasies More Than They Fill My Belly

In August, while I was in my farmermode, my grand-father was my role model. I didn't know any professional farmers, so my grandfather became the stand-in for the real thing. He was the person I secretly pretended to be when I was out there with my cardboard box (no wicker basket or English-style trug for me) harvesting tomatoes. I pictured my grandfather standing among his crops in his green cap and plaid shirt (with Vicks cough drops in the pockets). I remembered his rolling walk, his quick sense of humor, and his equally quick temper.

When I was kid, I always used to look forward to visit-ing my grandfather's "farm." It lay on a narrow strip of land behind the apartment building in Oakland where he lived. He tended that scrap of earth just as if he were still back in rural Idaho. He grew green beans and corn and radishes and squash, but tomatoes were his specialty.

I didn't visit my grandfather's garden very often. Every Sunday in summer, though, he visited us in Berkeley, bring-ing my parents and me bags of perfect round tomatoes, which he had picked green and ripened on the kitchen win-dow sill. They were perfectly tasteless, too. He drove them over to us in his white pickup truck that was forever stalling in city traffic.

What did my grandmother do during those summers? I wondered one day, as I stood in the kitchen slicing toma-toes for the dehydrator.

She didn't grow tomatoes; my grandfather wouldn't have let her. He considered growing vegetables to be man's work, like hunting and fishing. My grandmother hardly ever went out to the garden. She didn't go into the kitchen very often, either, for she wasn't much of a cook. She served my grandfather's tomatoes sliced, with white bread on the side. That was about it. She boiled the green beans and she boiled the corn.

My grandmother certainly didn't preserve or "put up," either. And so, though my grandfather was my role model for a farmer, I had to reach back beyond my personal history to find a prototype for my farm wife fantasies.

As I stood at the counter slicing those Early Girls for the drying rack, I thought of Ma in the 'Little House' books, or of a homesteader in a Willa Cather novel. I pretended to be one those strong, hardworking pioneer women, preserving for the long winter.

All I was doing, really, was filling an old mayonnaise jar with olive oil and dried tomatoes. The tomatoes would add zest to Paul's pizzas, but they wouldn't contribute substantially to our winter diet. The fantasy of "putting up," however, was so rich for me, so evocative, that I might as well have been packing up bottles of preserves, filling the root cellar with carrots and potatoes, and hanging strings of onions in the attic.

I guessed that in the fruitful month of August, many American gardeners shared this fantasy. "Maybe the dream goes all the way back to Thomas Jefferson and his vision of an agrarian America; a country of small farmers, independent but responsible, husbanding the land, acting intelligently, living freely . . . Why shouldn't the dream haunt us?" I asked myself. "It's a nice one."

Summer Beauty, Summer Bounty

That August, my taste buds influenced my aesthetic judgement. Nothing seemed more beautiful to me than a ripe red tomato. Or a yellow tomato. Or an orange bell pepper. The purple figs swelling day by day on the fig tree were even more gorgeous than the remaining dahlias, or the last of the cannas.

And I admired my neighbor's apple tree, noticing the thick branches studded with green apples. I told my neighbor how much I wished that such a fine old specimen stood in my own yard. Earlier in the year, I had walked right passed the tree, barely seeing it.

My mother went through a similar transformation that August. Instead of picking flowers for the table, she began displaying her homegrown eggplants in a bowl on the living room coffee table, pointing out how stunning the glossy dark purple fruits looked against the rough gray ceramic bowl.

And my father-in-law, echoing the behavior of my long-gone grandfather (a man my father-in-law never met) brought over bags of pears from his tree, not just because he wanted to share the bounty, but because he also wanted us to admire the green-golden fruit.

Chickens, Grape Vines and Dusty Oleanders

Part of the joy we all took in playing farmer came from going off on a little vacation every time we stepped into our gardens. We pretended to be somewhere else—somewhere rural and probably hot and dusty. Of course, we all held different pictures in our heads of where that "someplace else" was, pictures shaped by memories of real farms we had known.

Paul's father told me that whenever he worked in his garden he remembered the vegetable plot he tended in Alsace as a boy, during the Second World War. In those lean years, he grew potatoes and turnips to help keep his family from starving. As an adult, he indulged his passion for gourmet vegetables and fancy herbs. Still, the act of sowing and weeding and harvesting always took him back to his turnip patch in provincial France.

My mother said that when she cultivated her tiny vegetable garden, she remembered the communal farm where she labored (not always happily) during the back-to-the-land movement of the seventies.

I had no such recollections—which made my visions of "someplace else" less gritty and more romantic. When I tended my vegetables, I imagined farmyards I had driven past on the backroads of Napa and Sonoma counties.

Specifically, I imagined farmyards with oleanders. I thought of the long, billowing, pink-flowered hedges I'd seen edging vineyards. And I thought of a white-flowered tree-sized specimen I once glimpsed standing near a white-washed barn. Nearby, a white duck swam around and around in a kid's inflatable pool.

For me, oleanders evoked heat and dust and chickens and rusty farm equipment and kids on metal swing sets. My own garden would not have seemed summery to me without an oleander or two. Oleanders helped me sustain the illusion that my summer-garden was a kind of farmyard.

That summer, two oleanders bloomed in my garden, although the wet winter had killed a lovely peach-flowering one, which I mistakenly had planted in one of the garden's low spots. The white and the cherry-red oleanders thrived in the long back border, among mostly burgundy plants.

At that time of year, the border was a big, unruly festival of bloom. Near the cherry-colored oleander, a huge messy *Gaura lindheimeri* was an explosion of thin stems that moved like grass in the wind. At first glance, its flowers appeared white, but the pink oleander brought out the blush in the older blossoms. Through the tangle of flowers, strong wine-colored blades of purple fountain grass thrust up fiercely.

The white oleander bloomed at the other end of the border, with white-flowered oregano at its feet. Pale pink cosmos ('Versailles Blush') bloomed against a burgundy smokebush. The various annuals and perennials and shrubs mingled together, creating a sloppy and completely satisfying summer arrangement.

Obedient Plants and Lantanas: A Late-Summer Duo

In the purple border, obedient plant (*Physostegia virginiana*) began blooming among the artichokes, just as the hollyhock mallow, betony and liatris were finishing. The plants shot up four feet high on strong, ribbed, bamboolike stalks.

"Why are they called obedient plants?" Paul asked me.

I showed him the way the little tubular flowers along the tall spikes stayed put as I pushed them this way or that. He was not impressed.

"What a stupid name," he said. "Who thought up that one?"

"The other popular name is false dragonhead," I told him.

"Why is it false? What does true dragonhead look like?" he asked. And of course I didn't know.

Despite its puzzling names, *Physostegia virginiana* was one of the best plants in my late-season garden. Toward the end of August, the white form ('Summer Snow') started blooming in the peach border, beneath the lemon tree. Perhaps it didn't get as much sun there as it would have liked, or perhaps the white form is naturally floppier than its rigid purple-colored relation. In any case, the tall stems tended to fall over, and that year I was too lazy to stake them. The stems lay on the ground and the flower spikes twisted upward, creating a forest of shorter spires, one or two feet high.

Tidy gardeners would have scorned such disarray. But I liked the look of the pointy white flowers growing through the ferny gray-green foliage of a 'salmon' yarrow, and poking out of a pair of lantanas.

The lantanas were almost as outstanding as the obedient plants at that time of the year. There were two different kinds in bloom in the peach border, quite unalike one another and quite perfect together.

'White Trailing' lantana rambled about through the midborder decorating the ground with its small, lacy flowers. Its relaxed form was a foil to the obedient plant's rigid profile; its bright white blossoms an echo of the obedient plant's larger flowers. 'Confetti' lantana grew in a hillock. It had larger, cotton-ball-sized blossoms, each one a fruit cocktail of raspberry, lemon, and peach. The flowers popped up among salmon yarrow, repeating the peachy tones at a louder pitch.

This part of the border was at its prime in late summer. The coral *Salvia greggii* continued to bloom. Taller flowering plants included peachy cannas, Shasta daisies, and white coneflowers (*Echinacea purpurea* 'White Swan'). The coneflowers, with domed centers and reflexed petals, contrasted nicely with the Shasta daisies' more conventional form. The coneflowers' placement between the snow-white daisies and green ferns played up the greenish tint of its petals.

In back of this, daylilies and agapanthus contributed foliage, though by August their flowers had finished for the year. (The browning leaves of Siberian iris and crocosmia were less attractive.) A treelike apricot abutilon stood at the very back of the border, its flowers swinging like bells in the breeze. Around its base, ferns and white Japanese anemone (*Anemone japonica* 'Alba') crowded together. In August, the anemone was just starting to bud.

For years, I completed this late-summer picture with a few peach or cream chrysanthemums, but that year, when I was pregnant, I didn't have the energy to refresh the borders with new flowers. I simply enjoyed what was already there.

Summer Annuals

The summer annuals responded to the August sun with a vigor that was inspiring. In the driveway ribbon border, blue bachelor's buttons (*Centaurea cyanus*) leapt into flower. Daisylike boltonia was the only perennial still in bloom there. It flowered alongside the delicate creamy yellow flowers of a many-branching annual sunflower, *Helianthus annuus*, 'Italian White.' Tall wild fennel contributed its frothy green foliage and flat yellow flowers. And in front, the annual white cosmos, 'Purity,' added lacy leaves, similar to the fennel's foliage, and daisylike flowers similar to the boltonia's. The whole arrangement was cheerful and summery.

The annuals were mostly casual, tousled flowers. Their very ordinary, very nice appearance suited the summer garden perfectly and reminded me of why I liked to grow annuals.

Earlier that year, in spring, there had been times when I wanted to give up on annuals entirely. The pansies and impatiens needed water, fertilizer, and lots and lots of snail protection in order to survive. Furthermore, the spring annuals were small plants, tender little gems. They seemed slightly precious to me. Even when they thrived, they didn't make much of an impact on the garden as a whole. I wasn't convinced that they deserved all the fuss and attention I gave them.

But the annuals in my summer garden paid back neglect with beauty. They didn't mind heat and drought. All they asked for was prompt deadheading. In return, they bloomed endlessly and covered some of summer's eyesores. By late August, white bachelor's buttons had engulfed the ripening lily stalks in the rose border, by the deck, while big, airy cosmos plants concealed the drying oriental poppy foliage in the womb chamber. Since I was growing lazier by the day, I was grateful for their service.

Autumn Eccentricity

For me, September usually passed in a mad frenzy of planting and transplanting. New schemes normally absorbed me so that I hardly glanced at the rest of the garden. But the year I was pregnant, September passed quietly, without grand schemes and projects. As a result, I noticed details that had escaped me in past years. To my surprise, I discovered that several plants I grew primarily for foliage developed funny little flowers just when the garden was at its driest and sleepiest.

These flowers were inconspicuous. Among the poppies and lilies of May, they wouldn't have attracted any notice, but they added texture to the late-summer garden. For instance, the green aloe and the gray hen-and-chicks both sent up peach-colored stems that opened into fleshy, asparaguslike orange flowers. These strange flowers leaned through the front fence, toward the sidewalk. Meanwhile, in the back yard, the licorice plants in the burgundy border sprouted odd creamy flowers on the ends of long stems. The flowers looked like broccoli florets and contrasted subtly with the felted gray coin-sized leaves.

The largest and most outlandish flowers at that time of year were the acanthus blossoms, prickly white-and-purple spires that shot up seven feet. Then, almost as soon as the plants bloomed, they faded—as though the effort of producing those grandiose flowers had been too great.

When the leaves collapsed on their smaller neighbors, I knew it was time to cut down the stalks and chop back the leaves. This was deadheading on a massive scale. As I toted the leaves to the compost, I felt like a grand lady carrying a plumed fan.

The garlic chives in the peach border bloomed in August, too. Their flowers were the most ornamental of this oddball bunch. The round, flat clusters, dull-white and delicate looking, floated above the chives' strong vertical foliage. A big healthy clump of them stood behind a mound of gray, small-leaved hebe. The colors were calm; the textures were lovely: it was a quiet spot in a sometimes noisy border.

A Renaissance of Bugs and Bloom

As summer came to an end, a strange revival of spring occurred in parts of the garden. Some of the perennials that I'd cut back months ago bloomed for a second time. The hardy geraniums, the cape mallow, and some of the candytuft flushed with new bloom. Best of all, the iceberg roses put on a second display almost as spectacular as their first. The rosemary (which I hadn't deadheaded or sheared back) had completed its own private cycle of rest and also bloomed again.

This spring revival brought with it a new batch of pests. I hadn't seen a single aphid since May, but suddenly there they were, coating the calla lily foliage just as it was dying down.

I decided not to spray the aphids, since the calla lilies were fading anyway. Within days, the infected foliage turned yellow and shriveled up, leaving large gaps in the backs of the borders. Soon, however, fresh green stems with tightly wrapped leaves broke through the earth, looking just like furled umbrellas. In a week, the young leaves unfolded. The reborn plants were fresh and strong. Interestingly, the aphids didn't attack this new foliage.

Weeds and Other Aggravations

Autumn was difficult the year I was pregnant. By mid-September, I was growing awkward on my feet and certain chores were almost impossible to execute. Since I wasn't used to feeling so ineffective, my condition frustrated me.

Toward the end of the month, the dormant acanthuses sprouted small emerald green leaves. I knew from experience that these diminutive leaves would grow quickly into massive dark-green plumes. The acanthuses were threatening to choke the narrow border on the house's north side. I wanted to divide them before they took over, but I wasn't sure if I could manage.

Actually "divide" is not right the word. When I attempt to control the ever-widening clumps, I don't divide the roots so much as amputate them, chopping off hunks of fleshy tubers. Although technically, I could attempt the job at any time of the year, the task is easier when the plants are leafless.

So, eight months pregnant, I whacked at an acanthus root for a while. In the end, though, the plant defeated me. "Let the acanthus grow," I thought. "Let my garden become a jungle."

It almost did: I felt engulfed by plant life. The morning glories were scrambling over the fences on three sides of the garden now. For years, they had been trying to climb over the fence on the south side of my garden. Then, gradually, they'd crept through the yard to the east of mine and scaled the fence on that side, too. Now they were coming in from the yard on the north side. The only place they weren't coming from was the street, but any day I expected to see them slithering out of the sewers. Eventually, I was sure the strands from the different sides would meet in the middle of my lawn and shake hands.

I chopped back all the vines I could reach—the really bad ones, the ones that strangled the trees and tangled the roses. But by late September I was too clumsy to climb on ladders or crawl through borders, so I couldn't possibly get every strand. Reluctantly—furiously!—I let them go. I realized that some things would simply not get done that year.

The crabgrass was another trial to me that autumn. With the hot weather, it broke out like a rash in several places around the garden. The worst spot was beneath the hammock, in the ajuga among the brick stepping stones. The roots didn't come easily out of the dry autumn soil, it was tedious work and not very efficient.

As I weeded, I found myself remembering nostalgically how easily the onion grass bulbs had popped out of the damp spring earth. I told myself I ought to dig up the ajuga, get rid of the crabgrass once and for all, and replant the groundcover in clean soil. But I ignored my own advice and continued to pick ineffectually at the crabgrass.

I always worked on my hands and knees. I couldn't think of any other way to do it. As I crawled around the edges of the border, my belly—and the baby inside it—brushed the grass. I must have looked awkward, but once I was down actually I was fairly limber. Getting up again was the hard part.

In an upright state I looked like a gumdrop on toothpicks, Paul said. I preferred to put the simile in horticultural terms: I looked like a topiary. In my big green dress I looked just like a box hedge pruned into standard form.

One Question and Many Answers

One day in late September, our baby turned itself head-downward, to let us know that it was getting ready to come out. Only three weeks remained before the due date. In preparation, I bought a changing mat and cotton balls. The money I might have spent on mums went instead toward lots of soft, cotton receiving blankets. I also called around to the various diaper services to compare delivery rates. I began to live in a world dominated by baby matters.

During those last weeks, I worked in the garden less and less and lay in the hammock more and more. But I wasn't completely idle. While my body rested, my mind raced. I thought about the baby, of course, and I also thought about the garden. I thought about the baby and the garden together.

One afternoon, as I lay in the hammock—with my belly undulating wildly and the *Asparagus meyeri* waving madly near my feet—I was suddenly conscious of the plants and the baby living their own lives, separate from mine. "And yet I am responsible for them," I thought. "I am responsible for these lives."

And then I remembered Nigel. Poor Nigel. He was a tortoise, and the victim of a terrible tragedy. One cold night, when I was about ten, I allowed the heat lamp in his cage to burn out. As a result, before dawn, Nigel fell into a hibernation from which he never awakened.

"You cannot be relied on," my father chided me. "You're irresponsible!" For weeks I denied the truth. "He's only asleep!" I said. Until he began to smell.

Years later, I felt similar guilt about plants I killed. And I also went through the same denial, pouring fish emulsion over a red-brown heather and telling myself that it was only feeling peaked. Now that I had grown up, there was no one to scold me except my own conscience; no one to tell me—when I finally chucked the dead plant into the garbage can—that I had been irresponsible.

I knew, though, that I had reached a point in gardening where I nurtured more plants than I killed. I understood the responsibility of tending living things. And that sense of responsibility thrilled me.

"Is that why I do it?" I asked myself.

That September, as I rocked back and forth in the hammock, I returned to my old question. Why do I garden? I'd had nearly nine months to come up with a reason, but instead of finding one reason, I'd found a dozen. Reasons sprouted like weeds in the rainy season.

I'd discovered that I garden because I enjoy feeling like a beneficent, responsible adult caring for my own land. At the same time, I garden because I like pretending to be a child again, playing witch or Indian in a private, magical, green place. How can such different impulses create the same garden?

I garden because I want to play, to get dirty and scratched and bug-bitten. The physical act makes me feel alive, allows me to be sensuous in a frank unsexy way, eating apricots and sniffing lavender flowers, working hard, using my muscles, enjoying my body.

The brainwork excites me, too. I like fussing about the texture of the soil and messing around with compost. I like to get down on my knees and peer at ladybugs. I garden because I want to play 'science class' again. I want to return to the playhouse laboratory of my seventh summer and to my twelfth-grade Human Anatomy and Physiology class. I want to learn big words. I want to show off.

And I garden for power, because in my garden I can say, "This is mine. I want lawn here and flowers there." I garden to impose my will.

I garden out of vanity, too. I work hard at it because I'm too conceited to fail at such a public undertaking. I don't want to keep on killing plants. It's embarrassing. I don't want to go on creating ugly color schemes. What would people say? Instead, I want to learn which plant combinations work and how to create a harmonious whole.

I garden because gardening makes me feel proud; because every tomato I pick and every flower that blossoms adds to my sense of accomplishment.

I garden because the results can be beautiful. Gardening has shown me how to see. All those twenty-pound gardening books taught me about an art form I had never studied in college. Like painting, or music, or poetry, gardening feeds my soul.

And I garden because I want to live somewhere wonderful. My house isn't wonderful, but I can make my garden wonderful if I try hard enough. And I can do it without spending a lot of money.

I garden because I want to create a peaceful place in a chaotic world. I garden despite the drug dealers on the corner. And I garden *because* of them. I garden because I need a sanctuary.

These are the reasons I came up with that September as I lay in the hammock. The reasons were true reasons, yet I felt they were not the only reasons. Individually, they seemed oddly crude. Put together, they presented a distorted picture.

The reasons all seemed to cluster around the notion of achievement. I didn't believe, though, that gardening was only about achievement—about learning Latin words, and making lovely borders, and producing impressive bouquets. I knew that gardening couldn't really be such a selfish, soulless activity. It could not be, because it didn't *feel* that way when I was doing it.

Yellow Quinces

The quinces began to ripen in October. Some of the fruits were still green and fuzzy, but others were shiny and golden bright. The ripe quinces were five inches across and filled my hand. They were beautiful, though slightly useless.

The branches, burdened with ripening fruit, bent nearly to the lawn. I shoved patio furniture under limbs that threatened to crack. Then, as I lay on the grass beneath the tree, I treated my body the same way, propping myself up by stuffing pillows under my belly. Once I was settled, I wanted to stay settled. So I lay on the grass, buttressed with pillows, reading for hours, while the shade from the tree slipped away across the lawn.

The garden was quiet in October. Not many flowers bloomed—the white Japanese anemone were the showiest blossoms of the month. Some roses also still bloomed here and there. And, of course, the abiding Shasta daisies added a few more spots of white to the borders.

Mostly, though, the garden was yellow. Honey-colored. Saffron. Ocher. And gold. The dry lawn took on a golden hue. The leaves on the fruit trees turned a rich yellow. And the ripe quinces were a magnificent and indescribable shade of greenish, brownish yellow. I imagined that the garden and everything in it (including myself) had been immersed in a great jar of honey. That was how it looked to me. It had that submerged, otherworldly quality. It seemed suspended, like an insect in amber.

The garden seemed that way because it was hibernating. It was waiting for the rains to come. By October, it needed rain desperately. The trees were thirsty. The big shrubs were parched, too. My watering with a hose could sustain them only temporarily. They were waiting for a long, heavy, soil-penetrating rain to reach their deepest roots and give them new life.

In a sense, October was deepest winter. The first hard rain would be like spring. It would bring the promise of a new year—new leaves, new flowers, new fruits.

But for now, the garden was waiting.

The End

The due date came and went. The baby no longer moved as much as it used to. It was running out of space. Its wriggles seemed to be wriggles of irritation. I was growing irritated, too. I was impatient for that baby to be born.

To urge the baby out, I took long walks around the neighborhood. I walked until my feet hurt. And I jumped off the deck, again and again, landing on the grass, heavily. I jumped until I was out of breath. Nothing happened.

Then on October eighteenth, in the earliest part of the morning, something happened. I wanted to wake Paul and tell him, "It's happening, it's happening." But I didn't. I let him sleep.

I lay in bed as long as I could, listening to Paul breathing. Finally, when the sun was up, I got out of bed and went outside. I didn't want to go to the hospital until the very end. I wanted to stay in the garden as long as possible.

Between contractions, I paced around, stomping heavily —thump, thump—grounding myself, telling myself, "Here I am." During contractions, I stood very still, absolutely focused on what was inside of me, but also very aware of my garden.

The contractions grew stronger and closer together. I forgot about going to the hospital. I forgot about Paul. I forgot about the baby. I forgot about everything but those contractions. During an especially bad one, I threw myself down on the grass and lay there with my eyes shut.

I had never been so close to the garden. Nothing distanced me from it, not a metal trowel seven inches long, not clippers, not shears . . . or a pillow or a blanket. I felt my weight on the earth and its weight on me, and I wondered who was lying on whom.

When the next contraction came, I couldn't lie still. I got up and grabbed one of the quince tree's thin gnarled trunks, and stood, feet apart, swaying slightly, breathing through my mouth like a steam engine, doing everything I had been too self-conscious to do in the Lamaze class, all my embarrassment forgotten.

But even at the height of the pain I never forgot the tree. I never forgot that it was a living thing. I felt a partnership with it. It was there, steadying me. When that contraction ended, I lifted my hand from the trunk and saw the deep indentations in the flesh, where the bark had pressed into my hand.

During the next contraction, I focused on a cluster of leaves. I focused intensely. I was surprised that the leaves did not burst into flame from the heat of my stare.

I tried to remember what Karen, the Lamaze instructor, had said. "Don't hold back from the pain." That was it. "Don't shrink away. Don't hold yourself aloof. Let it inhabit you. Go limp to it." So I did.

I felt the pain. And along with the pain I felt the dirt seething with worms and invisible organisms. I felt the moisture in the earth climbing through the roots and going up the stems of the flowers and the trunks of the trees. I felt the insides of the plants, with their juices running. I felt the air around us all—around the plants and me—like the sky in a child's picture, drawn in blue crayon all around the dog and the person and the house, right down to the brown line of the earth.

I was out there for more than two hours, rocking back and forth in the grass, wetting myself with dew, gripping the tree, focusing on the pale green leaves. That tree hypnotized me.

Then Paul woke up and came out into the garden. By the time he appeared, I was almost beyond noticing him. He called out from the deck, and asked me how I was. I turned to him and raised my hand, saluting him. Then I threw up into a clump of agapanthus, and Paul said it was time to go to the hospital.

Giving birth is strange. Partly, you are passive. More passive than at any other time in your life. The contractions come and come and you stay sane by knowing that eventually they will stop coming.

At the same time it is harder work than you will ever do again. You use every muscle in your body, and all your strength.

If you garden, you know what I mean. A garden teaches you how to work hard and also when to stop working and simply accept what nature gives you. Giving birth is like that—it's a partnership between the force of nature and your own force. Nature and you. It's a powerful experience. You hardly ever get a chance to work as hard as you can in partnership with something huge.

Why do we make gardens? The act seems so extravagant, so illogical. Don't we have enough hard work in our lives already? Are we looking for more? Why on earth do we bother?

It takes a kind of courage. You have to learn to cherish. You have to dare, to take the risk, to bother, to care. To make a garden, you have to be able to love and to see yourself as capable of nurturing.

It takes patience, too. If the garden is to thrive you must commit yourself to it for years, for the creation of a garden takes place over time. Like a child, a garden has needs that have to be met, whether you feel like it or not, day after day.

You have to have confidence. You have to take charge and be responsible. You have to act upon the garden.

And you have to let it act upon you. Because it *will* act upon you. And will knit you together with the rest of the world. It will not let you stand apart.

The challenge is hard, but it is irresistible. To get dirty, to get involved. To act and be acted upon. That is life. If we stop accepting that challenge, we stop living.

We go on making gardens for the same reason we go on making babies. I suppose that is the answer to my question.

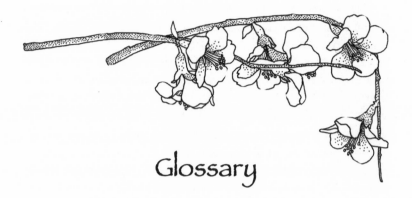

Glossary

An *annual* is a plant that sprouts, grows, makes seeds, and dies all in one year. In colder parts of the country, tender, cold-sensitive perennials, such as snapdragons, are treated as annuals. Conversely, in warmer climates, some perennials such as Iceland poppies are used as annuals, because they usually "bloom themselves to death" after only one year.

A *bed* is a planting area detached from fence or house. These beds, or "islands," are often surrounded by a lawn, gravel, or mulch.

A *biennial* is a plant that lives two years. The seed sprouts in spring, grows for a year, flowers the next spring, makes seed, and dies that second fall.

When a plant *bolts*, it grows quickly, makes seeds and dies prematurely. In hot weather, lettuce bolts, and becomes too bitter to eat.

A *corm* is often called a bulb. Actually, it is a thickened, underground stem. Its round shape is a bit squatter than a bulb's and less smooth, almost "hairy." Often from South Africa, corms do not require winter chilling, and will, in fact, die during cold winters. Corms are particularly well-suited to West Coast gardens. Crocosmia and freesias are two popular flowers that grow from corms.

Stem *cuttings* taken from perennials or the nonwoody stems of shrubs can be dipped in a hormone powder and rooted in sand or perlite. This is a good way to propagate more plants. Certain plants, however, root more easily than others. Fuchsias, candytuft and lantana are three flowers that are fairly foolproof. Cuttings are best taken in spring, before the plants bud. At this time plants seem to root quickly because they are full of energy and ready to grow.

Deadheading is the practice of removing dying flowers from a plant so that the plant will direct its energy into growing more flowers, instead of producing seed.

Dividing clumps of perennials, or bulbs, into smaller clumps is a good way of rejuvenating plants that have become too crowded or too big. It is also a way to acquire new plants.

A *double* flower has more than one row of petals and may seem frilly or even spherical.

In a garden with good *drainage*, water moves through the soil quickly. Plants get enough oxygen, even during heavy rain. Sandy soil, or soil with plenty of compost, drains faster than heavy, clay soil.

An *espalier* is a tree or shrub grown with all its branches flat against a wall or fence. The shape can be a formal and symmetrical, or more irregular and relaxed.

A *frond* is the leaf on a fern or palm.

A *groundcover* can be as tall as a shrub or as short as moss, as long as it spreads out over the ground with an even surface. Usually, however, it is a low, carpetlike plant. Groundcovers such as thyme can support limited foot traffic.

A garden's *hardscape* could include decks, patios, fences, walls, paths, raised beds, or any garden feature—except plants—used to shape and organize the space within a garden.

A *herbaceous* border contains plants—usually perennials, but sometimes bulbs—that all die down to the ground in winter and grow again in spring.

A *mixed* border contains shrubs, and other woody plants that do not die down to the ground in winter. It could also contain succulents, and annuals.

Mulch is any material, such as bark, compost, or even gravel, spread on the soil around plants to suppress weeds, conserve water, or simply to make the planting area look tidy.

A *perennial* is plant that lives two or more years. Unlike trees or shrubs, however, a perennial is nonwoody and sometimes dies down to the ground in winter, especially in cold climates.

Bagged *potting soil*, from a store, is best for starting seeds in containers, since potting soil has a fine texture and is sterilized, with no weed seeds.

Rhizomes are thick underground stems that grow horizontally just under the surface of the soil. They are sometimes called tubers, or bulbs. Bearded iris are among the most popular flowers that grow from rhizomes.

A *rootbound* potted plant has become too big for its container. Since the roots have used all the space in the pot, and cannot spread outward, they have started growing into a tight, matted circle. The plant needs to be repotted in a larger container.

A *single* flower has only one row of petals. Simple daisies and sunflowers are classic single flowers, although double versions of both exist.

A *standard* is a shrub, perennial, or even a succulent such as a jade plant, that has been shaped to look like a tree, with the stems pruned to a single trunk and the foliage clipped into a rounded shaped on top. Rosemary and oleander shrubs make fine standards.

A *succulent* is a plant with thick, fleshy leaves to store water.

A perennial with a *taproot* has a long, main root like a carrot. It is more difficult to transplant or divide a plant with a taproot than one that grows in a clump.

A *topiary* is a dense, small-leafed shrub or tree such as rosemary or boxwood that has been clipped into a formal geometric or animal shape.

Topsoil is the mantle of good, rich soil that lays above rock or poorer soil in a garden. Different gardens, in different areas, will have more or less topsoil. In gardens with very shallow topsoil, adding an extra layer will encourage healthier, deep-rooted plants.

A *tuber* is a fat, fleshy, roundish, underground stem. It is sometimes called a bulb, however it is not as hard as a bulb and can rot in a wet winter or freeze in a cold one. Dahlias are among the most common flowers grown from tubers.

To *underplant* means to set one plant beneath another in a garden. For instance, shrubs might grow under trees, or groundcovers could spread out beneath tall perennials.

A *volunteer* is a self-sown seedling. It could be a seedling sprouted from a plant cultivated in the garden the year before, or a new variety blown in from another yard, or dropped by a bird. Some plants, such as Johnny-jump-ups, red valerian, and hollyhock mallow, are more likely to self-sow than others. Of course, if a gardener chooses to deadhead a plant promptly, preventing it from setting seed, then it will produce no "volunteers" at all.

The plants listed here are the ones that seem the happiest in my garden. I've left out the ones that grow well for a year or two and then start to decline.

Indicates drought-resistant choices.

Abutilon 'Apricot Glow': flowering maple
*Acanthus: bear's breech
*Achillea millefolium: common yarrow
*Agapanthus africanus, 'Peter Pan' and 'Henryi'
Ajuga reptans: bugleweed
Alcea rosea 'Nigra': hollyhock
Allium tuberosum: garlic chives
*Aloe nobilis
*Amaryllis belladonna: naked lady
Anemone japonica: Japanese anemone
*Anisodontea capensis: Cape mallow
Aquilegia hybrids: hybrid columbine
*Armeria maritima: sea thrift
Asparagus meyeri: ornamental asparagus
Bergenia crassifolia
Boltonia asteroides 'Snowbank'
*Borago officinalis: borage
Buxus: boxwood
*Calendula officinalis: pot marigold
*Callirhoe involucrata: wine cups
*Canna
*Centaurea cyanus: bachelor's button
*Centranthus ruber: red valerian; Jupiter's beard
*Cerastium tomentosum: snow-in-summer
Chamaerops humilis: Mediterranean fan palm
Chives

Chlorophytum comosum: spider plant
Chrysanthemum frutescens: marguerite daisy
Chrysanthemum superbum: Shasta daisy
Continus coggygria purpurus: purple smokebush
*Coreopsis grandiflora: 'Early Sunrise'; tickseed
*Cosmos bipinnatus: 'Versailles Blush'; annual cosmos
*Crocosmia masoniorum
Dianthus barbatus nigrescens: 'Sooty'; dark burgundy
  sweet William
Digitalis ambigua: yellow perennial foxglove
*Echeveria imbricata: hen-and-chicks
*Echinacea purpurea: 'White Swan' and 'Bravado': cone-
  flower
*Erysimum : 'Bowles Mauve'; perennial wallflower
*Felicia amelloides
*Festuca ovina glauca: blue fescue
Fuchsia hybrida
*Gaura lindheimeri
*Gazania
Geranium: 'Johnson's Blue'
*Geranium: 'Wargave Pink'
*Geranium: 'Claridge Druce'
Helianthus annuus 'Italian White': annual sunflower
*Helichrysum petiolare: licorice plant
*Helichrysum angustifolium: curry plant
*Hemerocallis: daylily
Heuchera sanguinea: coralbells
Hydrangea quercifolia: oakleaf hydrangea
Hydrangea petiolaris: climbing hydrangea
*Iberis sempervirens: 'Purity'; candytuft
Iris, bearded
Ixia maculata
Jacaranda mimosifolia
Lamium maculatum: 'White Nancy'
*Lantana montevidensis: 'Confetti' and 'Trailing White'
*Lavandula angustifolia: lavender
Liatris spicata 'Kobold': Kansas gayflower
Lilium leucanthum centifolium: black-dragon lily

Lobularia maritima: annual alyssum
Magnolia stellata: star magnolia
*Malva alcea 'Fastigiata': hollyhock mallow
Myosotis sylvatica: forget-me-not
*Nerium oleander: oleander
*Osteospermum fruticosum: trailing African daisy
Papaver nudicaule: Iceland poppy
Papaver orientale: oriental poppy
Passiflora alatocaerulea: passion flower vine
Pelargonium: tender geranium
*Pennisetum setaceum : 'Rubrum'; purple fountain grass
*Penstemon: 'Elfin Pink'
*Perovskia atriplicifolia: Russian sage
*Phormium tenax: New Zealand flax 'Rubrum'
Physostegia virginiana 'Vivid' and 'Summer Snow': obe-
    dient plant
*Plumbago auriculata: Cape plumbago
Polygonum aubertii: flease vine
Rosa banksiae: 'Lady Banks,' 'White Banksia'
Rosa florabunda: 'Iceberg'
Rosa : 'Gruss an Aachen'
*Rosmarinus officinalis: rosemary
*Salvia greggii
*Salvia officinalis 'Tricolor': tricolor sage
*Sedum acre
*Sedum matrona
*Sedum spectabile: 'Brilliant'
Sparaxis: wandflower; harlequin flower
*Stachys lanata: lamb's ears
*Stachys officinalis: betony
*Thymus citriodorus: lemon thyme
*Thymus serpyllum coccineum: creeping thyme
Trachelospermum jasimoides: star jasmine
*Tulbaghia violacea: society garlic
*Zantedeschia aethiopica: calla lily

SIMONE MARTEL used to supply San Francisco Bay Area restaurants with organically grown vegetables. Now she writes and gardens at home, and spends time with her husband and young son.